AIDS

Other Books in the Social Issues Firsthand Series:

SOCIAL ISSUES
FIRSTHAND

| AIDS

Stefan Kiesbye, Book Editor

GREENHAVEN PRESS
A part of Gale, Cengage Learning

GALE
CENGAGE Learning™

Detroit • New York • San Francisco • New Haven, Conn • Waterville, Maine • London

GALE
CENGAGE Learning™

Christine Nasso, *Publisher*
Elizabeth Des Chenes, *Managing Editor*

© 2008 Greenhaven Press, a part of Gale, Cengage Learning

For more information, contact:
Greenhaven Press
27500 Drake Rd.
Farmington Hills, MI 48331-3535
Or you can visit our Internet site at gale.cengage.com.

For product information and technology assistance, contact us at

Gale Customer Support, 1-800-877-4253
For permission to use material from this text or product, submit all requests online at www.cengage.com/permissions

Further permissions questions can be emailed to permissionrequest@cengage.com

Articles in Greenhaven Press anthologies are often edited for length to meet page requirements. In addition, original titles of these works are changed to clearly present the main thesis and to explicitly indicate the author's opinion. Every effort is made to ensure that Greenhaven Press accurately reflects the original intent of the authors. Every effort has been made to trace the owners of copyrighted material.

Cover photograph reproduced by permission of © Louise Gubb/Corbis Saba.

ISBN-13: 978-0-7377-4028-8 (hardcover)

2008922026

Printed in the United States of America
1 2 3 4 5 6 7 12 11 10 09 08

Contents

Chapter 2: Living with AIDS

Chapter 3: Doctors and Activists Speak Out

Foreword

Social issues are often viewed in abstract terms. Pressing challenges such as poverty, homelessness, and addiction are viewed as problems to be defined and solved. Politicians, social scientists, and other experts engage in debates about the extent of the problems, their causes, and how best to remedy them. Often overlooked in these discussions is the human dimension of the issue. Behind every policy debate over poverty, homelessness, and substance abuse, for example, are real people struggling to make ends meet, to survive life on the streets, and to overcome addiction to drugs and alcohol. Their stories are ubiquitous and compelling. They are the stories of everyday people—perhaps your own family members or friends—and yet they rarely influence the debates taking place in state capitols, the national Congress, or the courts.

The disparity between the public debate and private experience of social issues is well illustrated by looking at the topic of poverty. Each year the U.S. Census Bureau establishes a poverty threshold. A household with an income below the threshold is defined as poor, while a household with an income above the threshold is considered able to live on a basic subsistence level. For example, in 2003 a family of two was considered poor if its income was less than $12,015; a family of four was defined as poor if its income was less than $18,810. Based on this system, the bureau estimates that 35.9 million Americans (12.5 percent of the population) lived below the poverty line in 2003, including 12.9 million children below the age of eighteen.

Commentators disagree about what these statistics mean. Social activists insist that the huge number of officially poor Americans translates into human suffering. Even many families that have incomes above the threshold, they maintain, are likely to be struggling to get by. Other commentators insist

9

that the statistics exaggerate the problem of poverty in the United States. Compared to people in developing countries, they point out, most so-called poor families have a high quality of life. As stated by journalist Fidelis Iyebote, "Cars are owned by 70 percent of 'poor' households. . . . Color televisions belong to 97 percent of the 'poor' [and] videocassette recorders belong to nearly 75 percent. . . . Sixty-four percent have microwave ovens, half own a stereo system, and over a quarter possess an automatic dishwasher."

However, this debate over the poverty threshold and what it means is likely irrelevant to a person living in poverty. Simply put, poor people do not need the government to tell them whether they are poor. They can see it in the stack of bills they cannot pay. They are aware of it when they are forced to choose between paying rent or buying food for their children. They become painfully conscious of it when they lose their homes and are forced to live in their cars or on the streets. Indeed, the written stories of poor people define the meaning of poverty more vividly than a government bureaucracy could ever hope to. Narratives composed by the poor describe losing jobs due to injury or mental illness, depict horrific tales of childhood abuse and spousal violence, recount the loss of friends and family members. They evoke the slipping away of social supports and government assistance, the descent into substance abuse and addiction, the harsh realities of life on the streets. These are the perspectives on poverty that are too often omitted from discussions over the extent of the problem and how to solve it.

Greenhaven Press's Social Issues Firsthand series provides a forum for the often-overlooked human perspectives on society's most divisive topics of debate. Each volume focuses on one social issue and presents a collection of ten to sixteen narratives by those who have had personal involvement with the topic. Extra care has been taken to include a diverse range of perspectives. For example, in the volume on adoption, readers will find the stories of birth parents who have made an adoption plan, adoptive parents, and adoptees themselves. After exposure to these varied points of view, the reader will have a clearer understanding that adoption is an intense, emotional experience full of joyous highs and painful lows for all concerned.

The debate surrounding embryonic stem cell research illustrates the moral and ethical pressure that the public brings to bear on the scientific community. However, while nonexperts often criticize scientists for not considering the potential negative impact of their work, ironically the public's reaction against such discoveries can produce harmful results as well. For example, although the outcry against embryonic stem cell research in the United States has resulted in fewer embryos being destroyed, those with Parkinson's, such as actor Michael J. Fox, have argued that prohibiting the development of new stem cell lines ultimately will prevent a timely cure for the disease that is killing Fox and thousands of others.

Each book in the series contains several features that enhance its usefulness, including an in-depth introduction, an annotated table of contents, bibliographies for further research, a list of organizations to contact, and a thorough index. These elements—combined with the poignant voices of people touched by tragedy and triumph—make the Social Issues Firsthand series a valuable resource for research on today's topics of political discussion.

Introduction

In 1981 the discovery of Acquired Immune Deficiency Syndrome (AIDS) created major political and ethical debates and led to fundamental changes in how society viewed love, sexual encounters, and partnerships. Since then, a positive result on the test for HIV (the human immunodeficiency virus, which is believed to cause AIDS), has gone from being a death sentence to being a condition that is fairly manageable and, in some cases, survivable—at least in the United States and other developed nations. While the rate of infections in the developed world has stabilized or gone down, much of the developing world is experiencing an epidemic. For those who cannot afford potentially life-saving treatment, an HIV-positive diagnosis is still a death sentence.

Nearly 40 million people currently live with the disease. The World Health Organization (WHO) estimates that the virus has caused the death of 25 million people since the early 1980s, making it one of the most devastating epidemics in history. In 2005, AIDS claimed an estimated 3 million lives, half a million of which were children. While medication has delayed the onset of the disease in infected patients and has prolonged lives, researchers are still years away from stopping the spread of AIDS.

Unfortunately, new, more effective medications may also have had negative effects in regard to the public's perception of the disease. According to Ann Christiansen Bullers, writing in *FDA Consumer*:

> The incidence of HIV infections began to climb in the late 1990s. So did the incidence of some sexually transmitted diseases—such as gonorrhea—that are closely linked with the type of behavior associated with HIV transmission and are believed by some researchers to even play a role in HIV transmission. Physicians and AIDS advocates believe these

events may be linked to the development of the AIDS drugs. A new generation of people in AIDS risk groups, experts say, now appears to believe that the drugs will protect or cure them of the virus and that an AIDS diagnosis today isn't serious.

Another significant obstacle is that the necessary drug treatments are expensive. "Treatment for HIV and AIDS patients cost the United States government $6.9 billion in fiscal year 1999, up from $4.5 billion just two years before," according to Bullers. The global cost of HIV/AIDS is about $10.5 billion annually. But each of the developed countries might have to donate that amount every year if the epidemic is to be adequately treated and contained.

Beyond the cost-prohibitive treatment of AIDS, in poorer and developing countries, the problems are fundamental. According to a UNAIDS/WHO report, "Prevention initiatives are reaching fewer than one in five people who could benefit. In middle- and low-income countries in 2005, only 11 percent of HIV-positive pregnant women received antiretroviral drugs to prevent mother-to-child transmission. And in African nations most seriously hit by HIV/AIDS, just 12 percent of men and 10 percent of women had been tested for HIV in 2005." Even after several years of increased HIV/AIDS spending, "for every person who began treatment, six more people were newly infected," according to the report.

The AIDS epidemic also has deeper effects on global economies. Shantayanan Devarajan, chief economist for South Asia region at the World Bank, writes that "not only does AIDS destroy existing human capital, but by killing mostly young adults, it also weakens the mechanism through which knowledge and abilities are transmitted from one generation to the next; for the children of AIDS victims will be left without one or both parents to love, raise and educate them. The outbreak of AIDS leads to an increase in premature adult mortality, and if the prevalence of the disease becomes sufficiently high, there may be a progressive collapse of human capital and productivity."

Making drugs more affordable will be key in the fight against AIDS in the future. And many believe that society's attitude toward the disease has to change. David Harvey, the executive director of the AIDS Alliance for Children, Youth and Families, writes that "our society is still plagued by the desire to label people as 'different.' The plagues of racism, poverty, substance abuse . . . continue to fuel the AIDS epidemic in America." In *Social Issues Firsthand: AIDS*, the authors provide personal accounts of AIDS in their lives, as victims, caregivers, activists, and physicians. These viewpoints illuminate the challenges of AIDS in the twenty-first century.

SOCIAL ISSUES
FIRSTHAND

CHAPTER 1

Testing HIV-Positive

HIV Is Still a Virus That Kills

David Salyer

In this selection, David Salyer, an HIV-positive journalist, looks at his own past and his struggle with AIDS and laments the new casualness he detects in the media and in those newly infected with the disease. AIDS, he concludes, is still the same incurable killer it has always been, and he urges his readers not to fall into the trap of ignorance. In addition to being a journalist, Salyer is an educator and activist living in Atlanta, Georgia. He leads safer-sex presentations for men and has facilitated workshops for people infected with or affected by HIV.

Y*ou will have a long and healthy life.* So I'm having lunch with my ex at Mama Fu's Noodle House and that's the message on the sliver of paper crammed inside my fortune cookie. *You will have a long and healthy life.* After living with HIV for twelve years, knowing firsthand the chaos this virus can do to your body, career, relationships and self-esteem, I had to laugh. I showed the message to my ex and he chuckled, too. "Great," I observed. "Now I'm being mocked by a fortune cookie."

Sure, there are people living long, healthy lives with HIV. Some have been positive since the 1980s, even before the virus was named. I meet them occasionally. Never taken medications; no opportunistic infections. Still working full time. You know who you are. There's even a medical term for you: long-term nonprogressors. Envious? You bet I am. To live with HIV for nearly a quarter of a century and not get sick . . . or go crazy . . . I hate you. Nothing personal. I don't know what *your* HIV is like, but mine is a mean, mutating, relentlessly versatile bastard foe—like having Freddy, Jason and Donald

David Salyer, "Testing Positive: To Panic, or Not to Panic?" *Survival News*, v. XVI, no. 3, May/June 2005, p. 19. Reproduced by permission.

Trump all riding shotgun. See, I was one of those guys who got infected and then progressed to AIDS in, like, four years, despite the positive attitude, lifestyle changes and a personal mantra: *I will not get sick.*

Getting Sick

People still get sick. Combination therapy fails. Oh, it's not widely reported—the American media is all over barebacking and sex on the down low and that so-called "new" HIV strain, but couldn't care less about the HIV+ folks who can't afford the drugs, can't take them successfully or never achieve the magic undetectable goal. Despite scrupulous adherence to numerous antiviral cocktails, one of my best friends has never—*never*—gone undetectable. Where's the press conference with alarmed public health officials announcing to the world that my friend's treatment failure should be a wake-up call?

News Can Make You Panic

How did you feel when New York City Health Commissioner Thomas Freiden told the world about a "new" strain of HIV that's resistant to three of the four classes of antiviral drugs and progresses swiftly to AIDS? Have you, like me, become so weary of shoddy AIDS journalism and exaggerated announcements by publicity-sucking public health whores that you are now automatically skeptical of any HIV reports by mainstream media? Is it even remotely surprising that, within a month of the arm-flapping about a new strain of HIV, scientists are now calling it *rare* and suggesting that one case simply does not warrant a panic?

Speaking of panic ... did you catch the news about Andy Bell, lead singer of my favorite European techno-pop band Erasure? Bell announced on his band's web site—how very new millennium of him—that he's been HIV+ for over six years. "Being HIV [positive] does not mean that you have AIDS," Bell wrote to fans. "My life expectancy should be the same as anyone else's, so there is no need to panic." *Whom are you trying to convince, Andy?* I guess it would be terribly uncool of Andy Bell to freak out, even a little bit, publicly. But it's odd, and frustratingly ironic, that Bell, writer of some of the most emotionally overwrought pop songs of the last twenty years, would make such a bland statement about living with HIV. Erasure's biggest 1980s hit was called "A Little Respect." Honestly, I have a little *less* respect for Bell these days because I think he's just pretending HIV is no big deal—and this attitude is starting to piss me off considerably.

Ads Send the Wrong Message

I'm also pissed off at pharmaceutical companies that continue to advertise their HIV medications in aggressively insulting and preposterous ways. Recent issues of *POZ, Out* and *HIV Plus* magazines carried full-page, *talking* ads for Bristol-Myers Squibb's protease inhibitor Reyataz®. Thanks to a microchip and speaker glued between pages, readers open the glossy four-page ad and hear a cell phone ring, then a carefree male voice gushes, *"Hey, hey, we're at the beach! Catch ya later!"* Across the page, two guys are playing backgammon in the dunes. The ad's happy-go-lucky tone suggests one thing: *Hot young gay guys don't need to worry so much about getting HIV because they can just go to the beach and pop some pills.* In other words, HIV is no big deal, nothing to panic about.

I meet far too many hot young newly diagnosed gay guys these days. Some seem a little too casual, almost dismissive about their HIV. *Scared? Nope, doing just fine here.* They claim, repeatedly, to be totally okay with testing positive. Some of them are so unnaturally okay with it that I'm tempted to slap them hard. But listen long enough and something real and human always slips through a crack in the faked complacency. One told me he just didn't want to end up looking like all those older positive guys with sunken cheeks, veiny legs and shapeless butts. *Well, dude, you might end up exactly like that.*

But even though your HIV fears are tied to your vanity, it doesn't make them any less legitimate. So go ahead, freak out. Cry. And do me a favor: try really hard not to give this godforsaken virus to anyone else.

AIDS Stole My Good Looks

I've got some of that sunken cheek thing going on myself—a slightly gaunt look that makes me feel like an extra in a low-budget horror movie—and I'd give anything to have my face back . . . and my ass . . . *especially* my ass. So I attended a forum on Sculptra™, the new injectable filler for people with facial lipoatrophy. A couple of treatments, dozens of needle jabs to the face—*it's a big needle*—and with a little luck, you might look something like the person you were before you started taking the meds . . . that you're still taking. Watching the demonstration on a live, HIV+ model, I knew it would take a dangerous amount of *Xanax* [anti-anxiety drug] to get me through that procedure. And my heart sank a little knowing that my next twelve years with HIV will surely include innumerable meds, more side effects and some kind of extreme makeover.

Panic. Don't panic. HIV is a big deal. HIV is no big deal. We seem to be getting a lot of mixed messages about the virus these days. How are we supposed to feel about it?

Personally, I'm annoyed with public health officials who make melodramatic, premature public disclosures about HIV, especially when it looks like they're just exploiting any new development to frighten people into practicing safer sex or quit having it at all. I'm disappointed that our government is doing less and less in terms of HIV prevention and education, having all but replaced the two with vague testing initiatives and recklessly inept abstinence programs that have no proven impact whatsoever on sexually active teens *or* adults. Any celebrity who suggests that HIV will have no impact on their life expectancy bewilders me—especially when I can count a dozen AIDS-related deaths of friends and acquaintances under the age of 55 in the last four years. And I'm outraged that pharmaceutical companies continue to promote their HIV drugs with the kind of glib tenacity typically associated with cell phone and soft drink advertising.

AIDS Is a Killer

Cancer is still scary, right? It's okay to freak a little, shed some tears and solicit prayers when it's about the Big C. Well, HIV is still scary, too—and not because a bunch of over-the-top public health drama queens tell us so. We know the stigma is still around. We know the treatments are frequently toxic, prohibitively expensive and *not a cure*. We know about the side effects—diarrhea, diabetes, the humps, flat asses, ballooning bellies and sunken cheeks. We know about the rejection—from employers and families and lovers. In our hearts, we know that HIV is still a big deal. No matter how chronic but manageable all those folks who *don't* have the virus keep telling us it is, HIV is the same hateful, killer virus it's always been, and we're not doing anyone any favors by pretending it's not.

A Pregnant Woman Fights for Her Baby

Kathleen Tyson

HIV-testing for pregnant women is becoming more common in the United States. It has been shown that treatment during pregnancy can help reduce the likelihood of the infection being transmitted to the infant during birth. Women who test positive under these circumstances may find that their wishes as a parent are overridden by hospital policies and state laws governing the care of their child. Kathleen Tyson describes her experience learning she was HIV-positive before the birth of her son.

September 17, 1998, is a date I will always remember. I was six months pregnant, and at 38 feeling a little old for the rigors of pregnancy, a full-time job, and the care of our ten-year-old daughter. But my husband, David, and I were joyfully anticipating the birth of our son. Then I received a call from my midwife at the Peace Health Birth Center. She told me my test results were in and asked if I could come down immediately and talk. This was worrisome. I located David, and we went to the birth center, where I was led to a private room. There the midwife told me gently that my HIV test had come back positive.

I was incredulous, then devastated. The next day, we consulted a high-risk perinatologist, who told us that his suggested course of treatment would be repeated doses of the drugs AZT and nelfinavir (a protease inhibitor). These, he said, would help to reduce the risk of transmission of the HIV virus to my unborn child. Of course, he added, I also would have to have a cesarean section at birth.

Kathleen Tyson, "In the Eye of the Storm: A Mother's True Story of Confronting AIDS, Fate, and the State," *Mothering Magazine*, September 2001. Reproduced by permission of the author.

I walked out in a daze. I had been feeling so healthy. Since high school I had been a vegetarian, practiced yoga, studied dance. I ran about ten to 16 miles per week, gardened, played with Faye. I was in the best, most vigorous shape of my life.

But that ended after I started on the prescribed drugs. Every morning, as I arrived at work, the first dosages would hit my bloodstream, and I'd be overcome by incredible exhaustion. The sicker I felt, the more I worried about the safety of the drugs and their effect on my unborn son.

Doctors Ignored Side Effects

My doctors brushed aside my concerns, telling me that the consequences of transmitting HIV to my son would be much more devastating than any possible side effects from the drugs. He added that children born to mothers who had used AZT were fine, even though he could not give me any studies to prove this.

I remained worried, haunted by thoughts of thalidomide [a widely prescribed drug in the 1950s that caused birth defects] and birth defects. Six weeks into my antiretroviral medication regime, having read everything I could find about AZT and pregnancy—and having found most of it extremely disquieting—I made the wrenching decision to discontinue the drugs.

Taking on the State

Today, [in 2001,] we're still in the middle of that fight. As our case has gotten national attention, we have received, in turn, an astonishing outpouring of support from people everywhere.

Soon after the first hearing, the local child-welfare agency offered us a deal: If I would agree not to breastfeed, the child endangerment case against us would be dropped, and we would be allowed to go on with our lives.

I refused. I did not want to be a martyr. And God knows, I don't want to lose custody of my son. But the issue of how to treat Felix and the broader issue of whether the state can mandate medical treatment for anyone's child are simply too important to ignore. I sincerely believe that light needs to be shed on this topic, and that the practice of ignoring the well-considered and deeply reasoned plans parents have for the care of their children has to stop.

My experience is not unique. I wish it were. I would not wish for any other parent to be in my situation. It's a terrible thing to have to make life and death decisions about the welfare of your child. But I'm the one who should make those decisions. No one else ever will love or worry about my child as I do. And with that knowledge to buoy us, I hope—and firmly believe—that we will prevail.

An African Woman's Quest for Survival

Chatinkha Nkhoma

In the following article, Chatinkha Nkhoma describes her peril-
ous journey from a good life in Africa to an uncertain future in
America. Diagnosed with AIDS, the author, a successful profes-
sional, is not able to receive adequate medical treatment in her
home country and seeks refuge with friends in the United States.
Unable to work, she becomes dependent on others to stay alive.
Nkhoma is a Malawi-born HIV-positive activist living in Mary-
land who is working to make HIV drugs available in Africa.

My life took a drastic turn when I was diagnosed with
AIDS in June 1999. I believe that turn began around
March 1997, when I began experiencing signs of the disease. I
didn't know at that time that these were AIDS symptoms. I
had chronic cramping, painful diarrhea, night sweats, burning
feet, and flulike symptoms that I mistook for malaria (and
treated as such), along with strange burning rashes, and what
I later found out was oral, anal, and vaginal thrush.

At that time in Malawi, where I am from, we believed that
the symptoms of HIV were rapid weight loss accompanied by
tuberculosis, shingles, and diarrhea. Since I wasn't losing
weight and didn't have tuberculosis or shingles, I ruled out
AIDS. I had prided myself on being sexually careful and even
preached condom use to my friends, though occasionally, I
put myself at risk by having unprotected sex. Still, I reasoned,
I wasn't at high risk; I dated carefully and didn't sleep with
multiple partners. But I guess that wasn't enough. I needed to
become a sexual saint to avoid infection.

Chatinkha Nkhoma, "One Woman's Odyssey: An African Woman's Quest for Survival and Dignity," *HIV Plus*, April/May 2000. Copyright © 2000 HIV Plus. All rights re-served. Reproduced by permission.

AIDS Was Fodder for Gossip

In Malawi we spoke about AIDS in whispers and as a piece of gossip.

"Have you heard? So-and-so is said to have died of AIDS. Eh! Eh! What a shame." We then sighed hopelessly and changed the discussion. AIDS remained a hush-hush topic, silently wiping us out.

In 1997 at age 35, I had reached a comfortable professional and financial status. I had earned a bachelor's degree in international affairs from George Washington University in the United States, had a lucrative business in Malawi, drove an expensive 4 x 4 vehicle, and was in the process of buying a big plot of land on which to build my dream house. I was gearing up for a high-level diplomatic job when lightning struck. When I look back I believe it was God's wish to rid me of the excess baggage that I was carrying. He was preparing me for my current activist life.

I was very fortunate that my family stuck by me. Unfortunately, while I was sick, my brother Mike, who had been the first in our family to be diagnosed with HIV, committed suicide. He purposely overdosed and died in his sleep. He had lost his wife to AIDS a year and half before. It was such a tragedy, especially because I was so close to him.

No AIDS Treatment in Africa

As in all other African countries, there is no such thing as treatment for AIDS or HIV in Malawi. When you get infected, death is certain. I estimate that less than 5 percent of Malawians can even begin to think about treatment. The average citizen's annual income is less than U.S. $500, and the cost of HIV medication [AZT, 3TC, Crixivan] is an estimated $1,000 a month, which makes getting the drugs a faraway dream that immediately turns into a nightmare for most of us. We have free health care, but the medical system has collapsed under AIDS, and private pharmacies have taken advantage of the situation by charging high prices, even for antibiotics. In Malawi people die of curable diseases faster than from AIDS complications.

My own savings diminished when I began treating my pre-AIDS diagnosis symptoms. Things got worse and worse until a final blow of *Pneumocystis carinii* pneumonia [PCP] landed me in the hospital in February 1998. I spent everything I had to stay alive. My doctor recommended that I take AZT and 3TC, the only drugs available [in Malawi] at the time. To help me out, he bought the medication with his doctor's discount. After two weeks of therapy, I began to feel better and regained my strength. By the end of the sixth week, I was back at work. For me, there is no doubt that without the drugs I would have died.

The Cost of Drugs Is Prohibitive

But getting my health back brought other problems. By the third month on therapy, I was running out of money and, to add insult to injury, our national currency fell, which meant higher drug prices. I cried so much when I heard, thinking that just when things were getting better, this had to happen. I felt so hopeless. In my struggle to keep taking something, I ended up following part of the regimen. That is, I reduced my intake of AZT to two capsules three times a day, with one 3TC pill. I dragged this out for as long as I could, and finally dropped the 3TC. I'm not sure if this had any physical effect on me because I had no way of monitoring my viral load or T-cell numbers.

During this desperate time, my pharmacist would open a bottle of medicine and calculate the cost per pill, selling me a day's or a week's worth. It was pathetic, but the will to live supersedes rational action. The day the cost of medication increased, I vividly remember the pharmacist and I spending a long time crying together in her office.

I couldn't give up. Taking the last of my money, I decided to use a complimentary airline ticket from KLM Royal Dutch airlines, and traveled to Maryland to visit some college friends. I hoped to do some income-generating activities and see if I could buy HIV drugs more cheaply (I had been misinformed that they cost less here). Three days after my arrival, I suddenly got sick and was taken to a neighborhood clinic. I immediately enrolled in its program. I couldn't believe it when I heard there were free AIDS treatment programs here. I wasn't sure I would qualify, being a noncitizen. And if I did, I would have to relocate.

This posed a very difficult situation for me. On my own, I couldn't afford to buy HIV medications much longer. No medications spelled imminent death. And I was ill and emotionally unprepared to leave my family and face AIDS alone. Still, I felt I had no choice, and my relatives pushed me to remain here.

A New Doctor Leads to New Problems

Because I had been taking HIV medications erratically, and because I didn't have a medical history with me, the doctor who first saw me at the Maryland clinic decided to take me off all medications, including Bactrim for my pneumonia— even though I had a T-cell count of 36 and a viral load of more than 500,000 copies. Back then, I didn't know better and trusted that the doctor knew what she was doing. I believed she would not put my life in jeopardy.

After a few weeks off medications, I began to get sick again and developed ugly rashes. All my previous symptoms returned. I was rushed to the emergency room with another attack of PCP. The irony was that I had moved to America to find health, and here I was dying. It was then that the doctor finally gave me Combivir (AZT and 3TC), even though I had taken it previously and may have developed resistance, and Crixivan, along with prophylaxis treatment for the pneumonia and cytomegalovirus. This time, I made slow progress toward recovery, I was now stuck with a high hospital bill and, being a noncitizen, couldn't legally work. Fortunately, the United States provides emergency medical aid for HIV patients.

It was during this long recovery that I met Pat Nails, executive director of the Women's Collective, an advocacy organization in Washington, D.C. She quickly briefed me on my rights as an immigrant, which led me to launch a grievance process against the clinic. This only further aggravated the clinic staff. But it taught me that no matter what or where, my health is my responsibility.

Starting a New Life

After the hospital setback, I faced the challenge of setting up some sort of temporary life and regaining my sanity. I adhered well to the medication, and my health improved. Within a month, my viral load fell dramatically, from more than a half million copies to 700 copies, down to an undetectable level a month later. It is still undetectable today. My T-cell count rose more slowly, from 26 to 76, to my current peak of 217. It is still rising.

I have been one of the blessed Africans who was able to get drugs that have kept me alive up to now. But the cost has been as high as one can imagine. I have lost everything, professionally and financially, by relocating to the United States. The irony is I cannot work here, but I have a decent job back in Malawi. Now I must rely on the charity of friends and strangers, and sometimes I am so broke I don't even have money for a bus ticket to get to the hospital, or to put food on my table. I constantly face eviction. Thanks to a number of friends I have made in the AIDS community, I have managed to survive. But this type of life strips one of dignity and is humiliating. The choice is obvious, but tough all the same.

Two years after squarely facing death, I have not regained my full health. And I don't expect to. I know that once you have AIDS you can never feel as well as you did before. Instead, I'm constantly having one problem after another. I am staying alive, but my body has had to deal with the side effects of the toxic drugs, even though I have been on them for less than a year. I have also had to cope with anemia and skin diseases that have occurred as reactions to some medications. So some days are good and others are pretty terrible.

New Complications

Right now, they're pretty bad. I'm unable to walk because of bone complications that have attacked my hip and other joints. I'm not yet sure if these are side effects of the HIV drugs or due to the disease itself. But, by reaching out, I've met other HIV activists and recently managed to enroll myself in a clinical study of drug side effects at the National Institutes of Health. It was a pleasant surprise to go to a clinic where the staff was so professionally courteous and compassionate. But it's also very frustrating not to be able to get around, since my current activist work requires that I travel a lot. By now, I somehow have a strong conviction that this state of my health is not permanent and will improve.

But what about my African sisters? Their plight is still being overlooked, just as it is for women all over the world. In Africa, women have been carrying the heaviest burden, being both the providers and protectors of their communities. Not only are women and girls more vulnerable to infection, but they lack the means to protect themselves. Traditionally, women must also care for those who are sick and dying, and now, for the millions of AIDS orphans. Through all this suffering, African women—positive and negative—are enduring the extremities of the AIDS pandemic with remarkable strength. Their needs and contributions must be addressed.

Sometimes, I wonder if it is worth it to live like this. But all in all, I'm grateful to be alive, and I want to do nothing else than work toward fighting this enemy, HIV. There are millions and millions of my brothers and sisters back home in Africa who don't have the chance that I do, and who have no voice. They are dead and are still dying. People like my late brother Mike, my sister, cousins, brothers- and sisters-in-law, friends, and neighbors. While we are wasting time debating who should get AIDS medications, families like mine are being wiped out. It's a battle I wish we could all join arms in, because only together can we conquer AIDS. And if we don't, nobody will be safe anywhere.

Telling My Friends

Sven

At a young age, the author is confronted with the loss of a parent, drug addiction, and testing HIV-positive. In this essay, he describes his struggle to hold on to his family ties and to his friends while battling drugs and the deadly disease.

One of the hardest things I have ever had to do was to tell my friends that I had tested HIV+.

I remember each and every talk I had with my friends, breaking the news to them. I always will. Some of them were heart wrenching, some of them were comical but with each talk that happened, I knew I was changing my friends' lives. I was the one who brought reality home by becoming our first experience of having to live, love and deal with someone who is HIV+.

And in a way my news marked the true ending of our careless twenties and we all had to grow up just a bit more, whether we wanted to or not. All of a sudden this thing, this circle of life, became so very visible in our lives.

Unlike telling someone that you have a cancer, something that creates itself in your body by itself, having to tell a loved one you are now HIV+ means telling them that you at one point in time either made a bad judgment call or decided to not use the wisdom and knowledge available to you.

There was a tremendous amount of shame and sense of failure I had to work through.

Losing My Father Hurt

Then my father passed away and I became the first one in my group of friends who lost a parent. Once again, I had the unfortunate honor of bringing our own feelings of mortality

Sven, "Telling My Friends," *HIV/AIDS Positive Stories*, October 15, 2004. Reproduced by permission of the author. www.hivaids.webcentral.com.au/text/st225.html.

closer to the surface while further ruining our sense of invincibility. Without sounding like a victim, I was a serious downer to be hanging out with at that time.

How fast do we really have to grow up, no matter how hard we fight not to?

The second hardest thing I have had to do was to stand by as most of those same friends decided to part ways with me over the last couple of years.

I guess in a way I ended up on the receiving end of the "three strikes you are out" law. You see, within a matter of 12 months my friends had to not only process the news of me being HIV+; they also had to deal with me coming clean about my drug addiction and finally about me losing my job. Not to mention losing a parent.

And what those three things achieved was that they made the balance of equality in our friendships shift. I went from being an equal partner to someone who is sick, unemployed and an addict.

From being someone that got called upon for advice and support to being told that I was no longer to be trusted or believed was a monumental change in the way I interacted with my friends. From being the one that helped out to being the one that needed help; friendships went from fun, carefree and footloose to being strenuous, serious and supporting.

And the balance of equality shifted.

My Life Was Marked by Loss

So while I was trying to come to terms with being HIV+, losing my father, being unemployed and a recovering addict; I also had to deal with issues of abandonment by my friends, my anger towards those friends and the resolution of all those issues in a sane and constructive way.

A lot of that was done through my writing and the publishing of my website. It provided me with a forum in which I could vent my frustrations and work through them by putting my thoughts and emotions into words out in front of me.

It allowed me to take an objective look as to what my responsibilities were in my friendships and in life and how to deal with my part and place in both those vortexes together and individually.

Now, with the last and final loose end in my life being tied up, I am allowed to close the book on a very important and big chapter of my life. And I feel the need to somehow mark the importance of that event in my life as I go forward and move on. . . .

Looking for Peace

If [my website] in any way, shape or form may serve as inspiration for another person in the same way as it has been the pinnacle element behind my survival and sanity, it will have made these last three years more than worthwhile: it will have made them necessary and welcomed.

For such a long time I have been trying to find resolution and peace with what has happened in my life, especially the people that left. By dedicating this as my official last editorial, I have finally found a way for myself to do the one thing that I needed the most but never really got: the chance to say goodbye.

Even though they may not have been physically present in my life for a while, their presence and our past together remained very noticeable. Which is why they are (almost) all included on this last email: allowing me to say goodbye and make them part of the chapter that is closing.

For others this will be the last time you hear from me as well. I thank you for having been such a comforting and understanding part of my life these last years. I send you my love and sincerest wishes for an amazing life.

Thus is the tapestry I wove,

My name is Sven.

I Was Born HIV-Positive

Kaitlyn and Cleo

The first baby born with HIV in Montana, Kaitlyn received special attention early on and grew up with a positive attitude toward the infection. She and her mom, Cleo, talk about the illness, difficulties Kaitlyn and her family are facing, and the challenges of their daily life. First, Kaitlyn talks about HIV from her perspective, then her mother offers her view.

Sometimes I feel like a pioneer. I was the first baby with HIV in Montana, and I was the first kid with HIV to enter public schools in the state. These firsts make me feel special.

My parents adopted me when I was just two days old. My mother flew to California when my birth mother called to say she was in labor, and she held me for the first time when I was just five hours old.

My birth mother died of AIDS-related illnesses when I was three years old. I know my mother and I flew to see her just before she died, but all I remember is sitting on the floor of the plane and eating Froot Loops. I wish I remembered more, like the sound of my birth mother's voice.

HIV has caused me a few problems with people, but not that many. My best friend's mother freaked out when we told her about it. My friend didn't have a problem with it, but her mother was scared. She thought her daughter could get it from casual contact with me. My friend and I still played together at school, but we couldn't go over to each other's houses.

My elementary school had a great nurse. She took me into a separate room so I could have some privacy while I took my meds. She knew I had HIV, but she didn't judge me by it. She just gave me my meds and made sure I stayed safe.

The nurse also came into my class to talk about HIV. She started in second grade, telling us this is a serious disease, "but you can't get it from being a friend." She added more information each year.

I switched schools in the fourth grade, and I haven't had any problems whatsoever at my "new" school. We talk about HIV in health class and in science class. Everybody knows I have it because I was on a CNN special. It's just not a big deal.

Her Mother's Perspective

We have a large family—nine children, five of whom were adopted and two of whom have HIV. Back in the late '80s, my husband and I read about HIV babies being warehoused, and we wanted to help. An agency matched us with Kaitlyn's birth mother, and we adopted Kaitlyn when she was two days old.

From the beginning, she was an absolute joy. She began talking when she was six months old, and she was using complete sentences before her first birthday. Everyone loved her.

When it was time for her to go to kindergarten, we puzzled over whether we should tell anyone about her HIV. One reason for our hesitation is that I remembered how a social worker had reacted when I told him we were adopting a baby with HIV. "I don't know why you're doing this," he said, "but if your kid ever comes to the same school as mine, I'm taking my kids out of that school."

We knew we didn't *have* to tell anyone about Kaitlyn's HIV status, but we wanted to do the right thing. In the end, we decided to tell the school nurse because, at that time, Kaitlyn was taking meds five times a day, and the nurse would be involved in that. We also wanted to make sure the school would follow universal precautions in case of an injury. The nurse was wonderful and became a very good friend.

We ended up telling her classroom teachers each year as well. Teachers never had a problem with it, and they loved Kaitlyn. She was smart, well-behaved, funny, and adult-like. She was the perfect little student, the kid that all of the teachers wanted to have in their class. They were always sad to hear that Kaitlyn had HIV, but they never gave us a problem about it.

We've had a different experience with Rahkei. He's eight years old and the youngest in our family. We found him on the Internet. We had decided we wanted to adopt one more child, and from the social services agency's description of this little boy, I could tell he had HIV. The web site said he had a chronic illness that required constant medication. If it had been any other disease, they would have come out and said what it was.

We went to Delaware to meet Rahkei, but it was another year and a half before we were allowed to take him home. By then, he was three and a half years old, and I believe he had been mistreated. His foster mother gave me a big supply of his medicines that had expired. I don't think she was giving him the medicine that had been prescribed for him, and I'm pretty sure he was kept locked in his room much of the time. It infuriates me, the way the system let him down.

The result is that Rahkei is seriously emotionally disturbed and has an attachment disorder. He wants the same attention that Kaitlyn gets, but he goes about it the wrong way. He doesn't respect other children's privacy in the bathroom, and he touches girls who don't want to be touched.

In the summers we have him in a special day camp for children with emotional disorders, and the staff is very nervous about him. They know children in these programs can bite, spit, kick, cut themselves, and spray people with their blood. Lately Rahkei has taken to spitting on people because he realizes that scares them—even though we know there's a pretty low risk that anyone's going to catch anything from Rahkei's spit.

During the school year, Rahkei is in special education. The staff knows about his HIV, but his classmates and their parents don't. It's not a big secret, but we're not going out of our way to tell anyone. Rahkei has enough problems as it is.

When CNN wanted to do a story about Kaitlyn, we wondered how people would react to the news that she had HIV. It had been pretty much of a secret all this time, and there was no easy way to say, "The whole time you've been Kaitlyn's friend, she's had HIV." But people surprised us by responding graciously to the news.

How will they respond to similar news about a boy like Rahkei?

CHAPTER 2

Living with AIDS

My Twenty Years with AIDS

Bruce Garner

In this selection, Bruce Garner remembers the beginnings of the AIDS epidemic and how the illness was—and still is—frequently used to stigmatize certain social groups. He reflects on the lives of infected friends who perished and on how his own struggle with AIDS has made him into an activist fighting to overcome the prejudice and ignorance that surrounds the disease. Garner is a National Episcopal AIDS Coalition board member.

The date was June 5. It was a Friday—and it was 1981. That day the CDC's [Centers for Disease Control and Prevention] *Morbidity and Mortality Weekly Report* (MMWR) listed the first cases of what would later become known as acquired immune deficiency syndrome, or AIDS.

From the start, the scientific/medical community would perpetrate a travesty: They called the disease GRID—Gay Related Immune Deficiency. In doing so they would make AIDS forever a political condition.

It should have been unconscionable to even think about connecting a medical condition to a specific group. Tay Sachs, [a fatal genetic disorder] has no reference to people of Jewish or Mediterranean descent. Sickle cell anemia is not, by its name, connected to people of African descent.

By 1982 people had begun dying in noticeable numbers. They all had diseases like pneumocystis pneumonia and Kaposi's sarcoma [a type of cancer] that did not ordinarily kill people. Time would reveal other exotic, nearly unpronounceable viral and bacteriological infections that caused dementia, wasting syndrome, diarrhea, and ultimately a death as horrible as any imaginable.

Bruce Garner, "AIDS: Remembering 20 Years," *National Episcopal AIDS Coalition*, September 2001. Reproduced by permission. www.neac.org/articles/000139.html.

39

AIDS Was Used to Label People

In the early years, those thought to be at risk were referred to as the four H's: hookers, homosexuals, Haitians, and hemophiliacs. Again, labels associated with people were used to identify a disease. It would be several years before we learned that the method of transmission of the virus had nothing to do with who you were.

My involvement began when a friend was having problems with his Social Security disability claim. Months went by. In July 1984 I learned that Tom was in Emory Hospital again, still with no decision. The doctor had waltzed all around a diagnosis of AIDS but had never written the definitive words in the medical evidence.

I got the proper medical information from Emory Clinic and took it to the Disability Determination Services office. The examiner said he would let me know. I got pushy; I said I would wait. The examiner went away for a short while, then returned with an approval.

I rushed to Emory Hospital to tell Tom. He could not speak. The tracheotomy tube was still in his throat, though life support had been removed. But Tom smiled when I gave him the news. His children would be receiving survivor benefits as well as his retroactive payments.

AIDS Killed Many of My Friends

Watching Tom take his last breath just before midnight on July 4, 1984, is permanently etched in my memory. That was the year that the modes of transmission of the virus were identified.

In September, another friend, Gene, was diagnosed with AIDS. That same weekend I began my career as an AIDS volunteer with AIDS Atlanta; in October I joined the board of directors. I have been on at least one and as many as three national and local AIDS service organization boards ever since.

For many years I lost an average of two dozen friends a year. I once kept a list. When it topped 200 names, I stopped. I lost one entire generation of friends, then made and lost another.

Even after the virus was isolated and named HIV [human immunodeficiency virus], infection and death continued. In 1986 Surgeon General C. Everett Koop called for AIDS education in children of all ages. And he called for the widespread use of condoms.

Once the virus was isolated, there was new hope that drugs could be found to fight the disease. The first, AZT, was a gamble. It was not clear what the dosage should be, how frequent, what the side effects were, what the long-term effects might be. It began with four pills every four hours around the clock. You'd be in a group, a pill timer would go off, and there was a mad scramble to find whose it was.

HIV-Positive People Had to Endure Harassment

During those years we witnessed people with AIDS being bodily removed from airplanes and left to crawl across a sidewalk to a taxi—if one agreed to take them. We witnessed housing evictions, not because of inability to pay rent but because of having AIDS. Some dentists, even some doctors, refused to treat AIDS patients. Ignorance and fear were the orders of the day. For many they still are.

In 1989 I reached a milestone age: 40, and time for complete physical exams. Instead of an HIV antibody test, I chose a T-cell [a type of white blood cell] count. If the count was below a certain number, I was likely to be infected. I was. There was no screaming or crying, no hand wringing. By that time I was well versed in the subject of HIV.

Later in 1989, the drug protocols indicated that anyone with a T-cell count lower than 500 should be on AZT. Mine was and I did. I washed down my very first doses with a Michelob beer—and started beeping every four hours!

New drugs came out. Some worked better than others, some not at all. Some people could not tolerate the side effects. More people died. I made new friends. I buried friends.

In 1990 Ryan White died from AIDS at age 18. His name lives on in the Ryan White CARE Act—now the major source of federal funding for services for people living with HIV/ AIDS.

AIDS Is a Major Killer

By 1995 HIV was the leading cause of death for Americans between the ages of 25 and 44.

In 1996 protease inhibitors and multi-drug therapies were introduced, bringing new optimism. For many HIV is becoming a chronic manageable medical condition. The pills keep us healthy. But I still lose a couple of friends each year to AIDS. And the situation in the less developed areas of the world is deeply serious. The drugs either are not available or are too expensive. In those parts of the world, AIDS still means death. It also means millions and millions of orphaned children.

Several years ago on a visit to Honduras for the National Commission on AIDS of the Episcopal Church, I sat across the table from four young adults, all HIV infected. There I was, with access to all the drugs available. There they were, with access to virtually none. Talk about guilt!

Educational efforts in the gay community in this country slowed the rate of new infections to a standstill several years ago, but by 1999 infections were once again on the rise. A new generation of young gay men had not been educated by the deaths of dozens of friends. Youth equates with invincibility; add to that the false sense of security drug regimens appear to bring and you have a recipe for disaster.

AIDS Education Is Lacking

Sadly, children rarely receive adequate education about HIV prevention in school, at home, or at church or synagogue. Just saying no has never worked. Kids need to know in terms they understand, explicit and direct, what causes HIV infection and how to prevent it. Talking to them about sex, teaching the use of condoms, will not increase their sexual activity. From the high rates of teen pregnancies and STDs [sexually transmitted diseases] it's clear kids are having sex whether we talk to them about it or not! The only educational tool school administrators seem to find safe is the AIDS Memorial Quilt—but that alone is not enough.

There are powerful, dangerous myths about AIDS and HIV. Besides the widely disproved myth that talking about sex increases sexual activity, here is another: No African American men have sex with men. None are gay. If anything, they are all bisexuals. Hogwash! The same lie is told in the Latino community, and the Asian. Those myths kill!

AIDS is now the leading cause of death in African-Americans between the ages of 25 and 44. In a recent study done in six large cities, nearly one third of the young black gay and bisexual men are testing positive for HIV—one out of three!

Truths About AIDS

If you take nothing else away, at least take the truth:

Take the truth that more than 20 million people have died from AIDS worldwide and over 8,000 more die each day.

Take the truth that HIV infects 40 million people and that number increases by over 14,000 every day.

Take the truth that unprotected sexual activity spreads HIV.

Take the truth that the virus doesn't care what sexual orientation, social or economic status, race, creed, or religion its host might be.

Take the truth that there are men who have sex with men in all racial and ethnic groups.

Take the truth that your children and grandchildren, your nieces, nephews, brothers, and sisters need to know that having unprotected sex can infect them with HIV regardless of the gender of their sexual partners. Talk to them.

Take the truth that 4.3 million children under the age of 15 have died from AIDS.

Take the truth that there are over 18 million children who have been made orphans by AIDS.

Take the truth that sharing needles also shares infection.

Take the truth that needle exchange programs slow the spread of infection without increasing intravenous drug use.

Take the truth that AIDS is not a divine punishment for anything anyone did or did not do. If any of us truly believes that having HIV reflects someone's worth as a human being, we had better be ready to explain why someone gets the flu or cancer or emphysema or leukemia or polio or Hodgkin's disease or sickle cell anemia or Crohn's disease.

The final truth I want you to take away is the truth of my survival. There are those who are surviving with HIV. There is hope.

And the truth that you can do something about HIV/AIDS: Learn about it! Teach about it! Debunk the deadly myths! Save people's lives! Maybe 20 years from now, AIDS will be a disease of the past.

A Family Copes with AIDS

Lesley, Daniel, and Tracey

This selection presents perspectives of HIV from a young girl named Lesley, her mother, Tracey, and her brother Daniel. Both Lesley and Tracey are HIV-positive, while Daniel is not. They each talk about the difficulties, taunts, and harassment Lesley has been subject to in school, and the fears Daniel nurtures about his family. Lesley's story is followed by her mother's and then her brother's perspectives.

I was born with HIV, but I didn't find out about it until I was five years old. It seems like I've been fighting ridicule and ignorance ever since then.

In elementary school, kids used to say, "Oh, I can't touch you because you have HIV." I remember one little girl refused to hold my hand during a game of Duck-Duck-Goose. She said her parents had told her never to touch me.

Later, the son of a local doctor told me his dad said I would not live past the age of twelve. I was ten years old at the time and pretty terrified. I didn't have that much more to go before I would be twelve.

When I was in middle school, I was walking around a track in PE [physical education] class when some girls came up and said, "Are you the girl with AIDS?" I said no. Technically, I wasn't lying because I have HIV, not AIDS. But the girls made fun of me anyway.

Kids talk about AIDS in a very insulting way. They say "you have AIDS," the same way they say "you have cooties."

After I started high school, a boy started harassing me in the hall about having AIDS. He called me AIDS Girl and said I got it by [messing] around. I went to the office and com-

Lesley, Daniel, and Tracey, *Living with HIV/ AIDS*, by Rebecca Jones. Alexandria, VA: The National School Boards Association, 2006.

plained to a school administrator, who talked with the boy a couple of times, but the harassment just got worse. His friends were saying mean things, too.

Finally, I told my mom I didn't want to go to school anymore. I was tired of all the harassment. She talked to the administrators and eventually got me transferred to another school. I didn't understand why I was the one who had to transfer. Shouldn't someone have forced the *harassers* to leave?

I tried to be quiet about HIV at the new school. I didn't tell anyone, but some kids already knew. One boy said I got HIV from having sex with football players. I complained to a guidance counselor, but she said, "We can't control what comes out of a student's mouth." She said ignorance is everywhere, so I have to expect kids to say ignorant things.

When the guidance counselor found out a local magazine was writing a story about me, she got mad. So did the principal. They said I had transferred to get away from harassment, and now I seemed to be looking for it.

But I didn't ask for the article to be published. The reporter called me, and I just answered her questions. Sometimes I wish nobody knew I had HIV. It really isn't anybody else's business. I was in elementary school when my mom started going to schools and talking about HIV and AIDS. Sometimes I went with her when she told our story, and I just got put out there. I really didn't have a choice.

Don't get me wrong. I'm proud of my mom, and I like going out and speaking with her. We're helping people get educated—we might even be saving lives—and we're helping reduce the fear and ignorance that surrounds this disease. It's just that sometimes I wish the HIV were my private business and no one else's.

Shortly after I transferred, a teacher at my new school called my mom and asked her to talk with her class about HIV and AIDS. My mom said she couldn't do it because she knew I wanted to avoid talking about HIV at the new school.

When my mom told me about the teacher's call, I thought about it for a long time. Then I told her to go ahead and talk with the class. I want this to be my business only, but I know our story needs to be heard. It might just save a life. Besides, I'm getting used to being ridiculed.

A Parent Shares an Important Lesson

I've been living with HIV a long time. I contracted it from my husband, who later died of complications resulting from AIDS. But I wasn't officially diagnosed until much later. Lesley was only four years old, and she was diagnosed at the same time. My five other children are not infected.

I can't believe the ignorance that surrounds HIV and AIDS. We're in our third decade of dealing with this disease, and sometimes people seem just as ignorant and prejudiced as they were twenty years ago.

Even my healthy children have been ridiculed. My thirteen-year-old has a friend whose parents won't let him go to church with us because we're known as the AIDS Family. My twelve-year-old has been called names at school pertaining to HIV and AIDS. He's not *in*fected, but he's *a*ffected.

In 1999 I started speaking at schools and community organizations. I wanted to educate people—especially kids—about this disease. I tell them about our family and what we've been through. I tell them about the medicines and the side effects.

Lots of kids don't worry about getting AIDS today because they think there are wonder drugs to take care of the virus. What they don't understand is that there is no cure, and what is one person's wonder drug might make the next person sick as a dog. My husband [Lesley's stepfather, who has AIDS] was in a wheelchair for years because of the side effects from some of these drugs.

After I finish talking, kids come up and hug me. They say, "We've seen the billboards, we've read the pamphlets, we've seen the public service announcements about AIDS. Now, after hearing your story, we really get it."

Being Negative Is Not Always Positive: Daniel

I don't understand why I don't have HIV. I was born from my mother's body, the same way Lesley was. I don't understand how Lesley got the disease and I didn't.

Some kids at school won't hang out with me because they say my family has AIDS. Even after I explain that I'm not infected, they say I *have* to have AIDS because I came out of my mother's body. . . .

I know I won't get HIV or AIDS, ever. My mom says if you're not born with it, you'll never get it unless you have blood-to-blood contact with someone who has it. I'm very careful about that.

I worry about my mom and Lesley and my stepdad all the time. I worry that they will all die and I'll end up alone, with nowhere to live. Once I had a dream about that, and I woke up crying. I went into my mom's room, crying, to see if she was still alive. Then I went into Lesley's room.

I wish a guidance counselor would sit down and talk with me about all of this. I was thinking about talking to a counselor, but then I saw what happened to Lesley. She talked to a counselor at her school, and the counselor told the principal what she said. Ever since then, the principal has had an attitude about Lesley and keeps giving her bad looks.

I worry that if I talk to the guidance counselor at my school, the same thing will happen to me. So I don't say anything.

A Support Group for AIDS Caregivers in South Africa

Danna Harman

Millions of children in Africa have been orphaned as AIDS-related illnesses took their parents. In many cases, these AIDS orphans have become the responsibility of their grandparents. This article opens a window into the difficult lives of South African grandmothers who are caring for children orphaned by AIDS and the efforts of one volunteer to help them cope through a support group. Danna Harman is a correspondent for The Christian Science Monitor.

The golden years. A time to relax. Maybe even indulge in a few luxuries. That's what these grannies dreamed of, but circumstances have been unkind.

Of the more than 11 million African children who lost parents to AIDS-related illnesses in the past decade, according to the UN, 40 to 60 percent are cared for by grandmothers.

Here in one of South Africa's poorest townships, Ingrid Moloi decided to help lessen the burden they face. For a handful of grannies—or go-gos as they're called here—her support group has become a lifeline.

"These meetings are about talking about what's inside our hearts," says Tabitha Mokoena, who has eight orphan grandchildren ranging from age 3 to 20 sleeping on the floors of her two-room shack.

"Sometimes when I start to talk, I cry," says Ms. Mokoena. "We all start to cry . . . about the stresses in our hearts. I don't know how these children will grow up."

Ms. Moloi, 33 years old, is unlikely to become a grandmother. Raped by her father at age 12, she contracted HIV and, a few years ago, was on her deathbed.

But, then, she says, her body began to respond to treatment. She gained weight, got up on her feet, stopped coughing, combed her brittle hair into a fashionable do, and came to Friends for Life, a local nongovernmental organization, for counseling. Soon, she became a volunteer counselor herself. "I feel," she reflects, ". . . like I asked God for a second chance at life, and when he gave it to me, I needed to make a difference."

Caring for the Caretakers

Moloi soon realized that not only the sick needed help, but so did their caretakers. And that, five years ago, is when she put a small notice on the community center bulletin board, calling for a grannies get together.

The go-gos meet twice a week. On Wednesdays they go to a nearby vegetable garden and plant together, dividing and taking home what they manage to grow—a small but invaluable supplement to diets consisting mostly of cornmeal.

And on Fridays, they gather at the Friends for Life offices, pull plastic chairs into a circle and, guided by Moloi, speak about events of the week at home.

Sometimes someone has advice about how to help kids with homework, or how to maneuver through government bureaucracy to apply for orphan grants ($33 a child a month). Mostly though, they just offer each other empathy and friendship.

Moloi, boisterous, loving, dramatic and irritable all at once, does not let any conversation here become too bogged down in self-pity. "Please, please, let's not forget how strong we are," she repeats like a mantra.

A New Year's Party

Today is the grannies' New Year's party, and the go-gos are dressed in their finest for a feast provided by Moloi. Mokoena wears a fancy traditional hat. Johanna Mlambo sports a necklace of broken pearls that her employer gave her. Tryphina Sibiya—the self-anointed babe of the crowd—has come in fishnet stockings. "These were expensive stockings. But I don't want to look old," she explains, flipping her short hair.

Ms. Sibiya once had six children—today all but one are dead. She lives with her last remaining son, Thoko, and three orphan grandchildren. Thoko works, she says, but she does not know where. He comes home only to sleep. "He does not help me. I ask him to but he doesn't want to. What can I do?" she asks.

One o'clock comes and goes but Moloi, who has bought the entire holiday meal out of her own $340-dollar-a-month salary, is running late, foiled by an electricity outage that has interrupted her cooking.

Soon, Sibiya begins to sing, first slowly, and then, her voice rising, she stands up and belts out a Zulu classic: "I will never forget my God." Mlambo joins in, singing alto. Mokoena gets up on her feet and shuffle-dances across the room. Someone yells Hallelujah, and for the next hour, the group sings together, one song stumbling into the next. They wave their arms, and rock side to side in unison, their voices intertwining. "Your child is my child," they melodize. "God is making wonders, he hears our sick children," they croon.

At 3 P.M., Moloi, in her best party dress, rushes in—Friends for Life staff hauling in pots of food and panting behind her. Soon, everyone is seated around a long table, piling massive quantities of rice, fried chicken, beets, and cabbage smothered with mayo onto one another's plates. There is sudden silence as the women tuck in, washing it all down with grape Fanta.

Around the table, two grannies, sick with AIDS, can barely manage to eat a bite. Most of the others can't finish either— scraping leftovers into plastic bags they brought from home.

Remaining Strong Together

As the eating frenzy subsides, Moloi stands up to give a blessing. "It is an honor to lead you grannies . . . even with all your complaining and crying," she begins, teasing. "I wish there were bigger presents I could give you, but I give you all my respect." The grannies nod and cry out, "Yes."

"Some in our group have died this year, but we remain strong here, together," continues Moloi.

"The grannies of today are not the grannies of yesterday. You are still bathing the children. You are still struggling," says Moloi, her voice rising like a preacher. "I know one day you will go . . . . I know one day I will go. But we have time now. We must fill that time and work for the children." "Amen," cry the grannies, dabbing away tears.

One by one, the elderly ladies stand and give testimony to the young woman they call Mama. "We tell jokes here, and we laugh," says Sibiya. "This is our only time to reflect. And we thank you Mama, for making this other home for us."

Moloi is beaming. A slow improvised song begins: "Thank you, God, for small pleasures," they all sing.

Over in the corner of the room, Mokoena is snoozing, exhausted from the food and the general excitement.

Soon, she will have to go back to the kids. But for the moment, she is in no hurry.

My Life Has Become More Urgent

Paula Peterson

Paula Peterson, despite leading the regular life of devoted wife and mother, became mysteriously infected with HIV. After the shock and early despair, she has learned to live with her illness and describes how her life is more focused on the things she loves: raising her child and writing. Peterson is the author of Penitent, with Roses: An HIV+ Mother Reflects.

When I first learned that I had full-blown AIDS, I thought I was going to die the next day. I felt like my future had been cut off. That was nine or ten months ago. Time now is broken up into "before the diagnosis" and "after the diagnosis." Every day is really weighty. Rather than months, I feel it in days. It just feels like every hour, every minute counts. It's not that I feel that I don't have a future exactly. It's just very uncertain. But I no longer wake up and think I am going to die that day.

It took a long time before I was diagnosed with AIDS. I was very run-down after the baby was born. I was tired—but all new mothers are tired. Then I got very sick with sinusitis. I had very high fevers, night sweats. The doctor gave me antibiotics. But I just really didn't get better. Then I developed a nasty ear infection. And I had an awful cough. I had lost weight. At that point I was beginning to think, there is something going on here.

Doctors Were Reluctant to Suggest I Had AIDS

I kept going back and forth to doctors and nurse practitioners at a major hospital. They even did a pulmonary function test

Paula Peterson, *Focus on Living: Portraits of Americans with HIV and AIDS*, by Roslyn Banish. Essay on Paula Peterson and Griff Butler pp. 40–49. Amherst, MA: University of Massachusetts Press, 2003. © 2003 Roslyn Banish. Reproduced by permission.

and ct scans of my head. They did various blood tests. Nothing showed up. But they did not give me an HIV test. I remember one doctor who said, "Well, do you think you are depressed?" And I said, "Yeah, I'm really depressed because I've been sick for so long." Finally four months later my doctor said, "Why don't you take an HIV test? You don't have anything that would lead me to think you had AIDS but why don't you try it to rule it out?"

I really didn't think AIDS was a possibility, but I was still really frightened of the test. I had an appointment with my doctor two weeks after the test. I remember trying to call his office before the two weeks to find out the test results. I spoke to a nurse who said, "Oh, don't worry about it. Just wait to see your doctor." And so I finally saw my doctor at the scheduled appointment. I had to remind him I was waiting for the results of my HIV test. He went out of the room and came back and said. "I have some really harsh news for you." And that's how I found out.

How Did I Get Infected?

My husband and my son were tested. I was very worried about my son because I breast-fed him up until the morning of my diagnosis. They showed up negative. That is a miracle! How I got AIDS remains a mystery. I have been with my husband basically since 1989. I contacted boyfriends I had before my marriage and they are fine. And I know it wasn't drugs. It's kind of a mystery I have to let go of.

I was such a basket case when I was first diagnosed that I really don't know how I pulled myself out of it. I think it was taking care of my son that helped me. I realized I had to be a mother to him again and that was one thing that helped get me off the couch. And then, of course, gradually having my physical strength return and doing well on the medications that were given to me. I've been on the protease inhibitors and I've done very well on them. I'm really feeling almost like my old self.

I think I have always had some inner strength. I've never had to go through anything as bad as this in my life. But I haven't fallen apart either. I love to read. I write. I've been going to a therapist once a week and that helps.

My Family Has Given Me Their Support

My husband has been wonderful. And my parents were supportive from the beginning. At first my mother was in a state of shock, of course, especially when I didn't know if my baby was sick. That was the hardest thing to go through, the first couple of weeks before we knew my son's test results. My parents moved from the Midwest to be closer to me so they could help out. When I first got diagnosed, they were here almost every day. I was also very depressed, just out of my mind with worry. So they really were helping me. But it's hard for them to live here. It's not their hometown and they feel out of place.

Now I feel healthy again, and I am able to take care of my son myself. I've also been reaching out to people more and have started to make some friends here. Just having a baby helped. I know other women with babies. They don't have HIV, but they have all been very supportive of me. I don't have any close friends with AIDS that I can share this with. That part is missing in my life right now.

For me to dare to make plans for the future is remarkable. I had barely started dreaming and making plans about my son when I got sick. So maybe the things I am dreaming about are what every mother dreams about. My husband and I both love to hike. So we dream of the day when our son is old enough to backpack. I dream about teaching him to read and to love books. But I think that would have always been there too, illness or no illness. I've been discussing what schools are best for my son. We are making plans for a vacation. We're talking about buying a house. Just normal everyday plans. Things that families do. I just try to live like I always did live, pre-diagnosis.

My Downfall Was Ignorance

When I look back on what happened to me, what caused my "downfall," it was just ignorance, thinking that someone like me couldn't get this disease. "A nice, white, middle-class girl can't get HIV!" That's why the doctors didn't suggest earlier that I be tested. But even if you aren't a drug user or a gay man, you can get HIV. I believe that pregnant women should be tested routinely. These are things they can do now for pregnant women with HIV. I was very lucky with [my son] Benjamin. And he got lucky. The fact that I had a C-section [cesarean birth] helped protect him, even though at the time I hated giving birth this way.

If I had known I was sick, I don't think I would have made the choice to have a child. So I feel lucky that I have a son and that he is healthy. I guess my biggest fear is that he won't know me. That I won't be alive long enough for him to really know me. And so that makes me more determined to stay well.

Four Years Later

It has been five years since I was diagnosed. Although in many ways my life has remained the same, from an emotional and psychological perspective I am light-years away from the woman I was then. In those years my health has improved immensely. My T cells [a type of white blood cell] hover between 500 and 600, which is considered to be a normal range and puts me out of the danger zone for opportunistic infections, and my viral load has remained undetectable. I've switched to a protease inhibitor that is easier to take. Aside from that, my combination is basically the same. I'm lucky. I haven't had any serious illnesses and I live a virtually normal life, except for the fact that I have to take drugs every day and go to the doctor frequently.

Medications Take a Toll on My Appearance

The only real physical complaint I have right now is cosmetic—my body has changed in some drastic ways due to a peculiar side effect of the drugs called lipodystrophy, a condition that affects the way fat is distributed on the body. My arms and legs are much more wasted . . . , my face is thinner, and my waist is thicker. There's not much I can do about this, and I suppose I'm lucky because I don't have the internal correlates that often go along with this condition—high lipid and cholesterol levels, or in some cases diabetes. I feel ashamed of being so vain, and I know I should be grateful just to be alive and healthy and forget about my looks, but I can't help it!. . . I long for my fuller face and more youthful appearance—even though I'm much healthier now than I was then, appearances notwithstanding.

I've changed in other ways besides the physical. Nowadays I consider myself to be a part of mainstream life—meaning that I don't feel as isolated by my disease and I feel I can participate in almost anything that [HIV] negative people can do. In fact, I'm proud of the fact that I'm in much better shape than some of my [HIV] negative friends! I assume, like everybody else, that I will live to see my child grow up, and that I have work to do in the world, that I have something valuable to contribute, that I can be productive and not just a burden to society. Whether my assumptions are ill founded or not, only time will tell, but I think it is healthy to live this way.

The most essential aspect of my existence boils down to two things: raising my child and writing. And I do plenty of time on both fronts. Ben is a happy, healthy, well-adjusted six-year-old boy, very intelligent and active and curious. I've grown to love being home with him. I wouldn't have missed these years, although if you had asked me what I thought of stay-at-home mothers before he was born, I would have replied contemptuously. Being forced to stay home because of HIV helped me to see what was most meaningful for me. I don't feel at all guilty about still being on disability. I've made a lot of valuable use of my time, so I don't feel I've been wasting the government's money.

My Writing Has Gained Urgency

The other main part of my life is my writing. In the last five years I've become much more disciplined about my craft, much more focused on it. Again, HIV may have played a part here—I feel more of an urgency to write, more aware of death. And having a child constricts you a bit, too, forces you to keep more regular habits. So I credit Ben a lot in turning me into a "real" writer.

I just had my first book published, *Penitent, with Roses: An HIV+ Mother Reflects*, and I have a new collection of short stories about HIV positive mothers which I'm hoping to get published. I have all sorts of long-term plans as a writer. I don't intend to always write about HIV either. One of the luxuries of being healthy now is that I feel I can branch out to other topics—take my place in the literary community, in other words, as I've taken my place in the parenting community.

I've changed in other ways, too. In the last five years I've done lots of volunteer work, including working on the San Francisco AIDS Foundation hotline and lobbying in Washington, D.C. I also have just started tutoring kids to read, and I work at my son's school. It's funny. This urge to give back, to contribute, happens to a lot of people with HIV. It's not that I consider myself a "do-gooder." I'm still mainly a selfish type—you have to be when you're a writer—but for some mysterious reason I found myself attracted to volunteering.

AIDS Is Not a Curse

I still get depressed from time to time. I can be compulsive, too, a big worrier, and I get irritated about petty things. I suffer doubly when I'm in a bad mood because I feel guilty about the depression. I feel like since I've been granted this miracle of good health, I should be grateful and make good use of my time, not waste a moment. I was talking with another HIV positive friend of mine recently about this pressure to live in an elevated or a particularly evolved way. That's part of the myth of being seriously ill, that we turn into saints somehow. And of course we don't.

Essentially, though, I'm a joyful person, and I'm ambitious, too. I don't feel like a "cursed" person like I did five years ago. . . . In 1997, I was standing precariously on the sidelines of life, waiting to see what would happen to me and trying to hold myself together. Now I feel like a full-fledged participant, and that means I fail or succeed in ways that are much like everybody else, that sometimes I'm good at living and sometimes I'm not. I like not being so "special" anymore. I like having the same chances everybody else does.

CHAPTER 3

Doctors and Activists
Speak Out

The AIDS Epidemic and Politics

Gregg Gonsalves

In the following article, the author relates how he feels let down by the current AIDS activist movement, which, he suggests, has become less and less politicized, retreating instead into the non-governmental organization (NGO) sector. He suggests bringing AIDS back to the forefront of politics and policy making, since AIDS, and the fight against it, is primarily a political matter not a private one. Gregg Gonsalves is a writer and an AIDS activist.

I told a few friends the other day that I was worried that I was turning into a shrieking harpy. There is no doubt that I have been horribly angry for the past 15 years. I have watched the AIDS epidemic flourish, mow down friends, family and colleagues, and, despite the vast sums of money and hives of activity devoted to combating the disease, new infections erupt in the millions, and millions more die horrible, painful deaths each year.

I do blame my government, other governments, drug companies, conservative religious institutions, and a rogue's gallery of other villains, but, lately, I can't help but think of my own role, our community's role in perpetuating the epidemic. I've written about this phenomenon before, but I am still stuck thinking about this, largely because despite my attempts to provoke a conversation in the HIV/AIDS activist community about how we do this work, nothing seems to change very much in our modus operandi.

The AIDS epidemic has everything, in [Canadian feminist writer] Margaret Atwood's words, "to do with power: who's

Gregg Gonsalves, "Rage Against the Machine: Anti-Politics and the AIDS Epidemic," *Treatment Issues: Newsletter of Current Issues in HIV/AIDS*, December 2005. Copyright © 2005 Treatment Issues. Reproduced by permission. www.aegis.org/pubs/gmhc/2005/ GM191201.html.

got it, who wants it, how it operates; in a word, who's allowed to do what to whom, who gets what from whom, who gets away with it and how." AIDS activists knew this once, the rallying cry of [AIDS activist group] ACT UP was that AIDS is a political crisis; we know this is still true particularly in places where the fight is conceived as an essentially political one: by South Africa's Treatment Action Campaign [TAC], by Russia's Front AIDS, by Thailand's Thai Drug Users' Network, by Costa Rica's Agua Buena Human Rights Association.

Don't get me wrong, I do believe that AIDS is recognized as a political crisis by many, many people. Think of the dozens of sign-on letters written and circulated, the meetings we attend to pound on the table, the reports, the press releases demanding this, demanding that. However, I have the sickening feeling that there has been a tremendous domestication of our political resistance—we trade on the legacy of our activist past or the reputation of our fiercest living champions, but as a movement, we have become a paper tiger.

Gay Activists Are Not Being Heard

Let's take the United Nations General Assembly Special Session [UNGASS] on HIV/AIDS in New York in May 2006 where governments came to boldly lie about their records in fighting AIDS and make hundreds of new, empty promises. UNAIDS [the Joint United Nations Programme on HIV/AIDS] staged a series of consultations leading up to this gathering to develop a framework to achieve universal access to HIV prevention, care and treatment by 2010. Activists were handpicked by UNAIDS to attend most of these consultations, where UN and government officials listened to the needs of people living with HIV/AIDS, of sex workers, drug users, women, men-who-have-sex with men and other "vulnerable" populations, wrote them up in reports and issued the findings in glossy newsletters put together just for the occasion. The UNGASS meeting will culminate in yet another political declaration on HIV/AIDS, based in part on these consultations and more centrally on negotiations with the governments that compose the UN's membership on what they can agree to support. Tremendous amounts of energy, money and time have been invested in these processes over the past six months. I was part of the "Global Steering Committee" on Universal Access and attended three meetings and helped to develop pages and pages of input for UNAIDS, hundreds of my colleagues have been busy finalizing "shadow reports," deciding who would go to New York City, who would be selected to speak at the UN, organizing satellite events to highlight important issues. Will anyone listen to us? Does anyone care what we have to say?

Has anyone asked why the hell we're devoting millions of dollars and hours to this process, when the previous UNGASS in 2001 resulted in a "Declaration of Commitment," which was honored neither in word nor deed? What are the opportunity costs for activists that are now hip deep in this exercise? What work hasn't been done or could have been done with this time, this money? The UN system is a system made for and by governments. Why are we engaging with a system in which we are not represented and [that] is beholden not to us but to its member states? Yes, "the international community must do more about HIV." But the international community doesn't exist as an institution; there are countries, and countries have leaders. Imagine if all these resources expended by the community alone for this meeting in New York City had been devoted to national campaigns demanding that governments honor what they promised five years ago? Or towards building real infrastructures for national, regional and international advocacy on HIV/AIDS? Or training each other on how to push for political change?

I can hear [founder of Treatment Action Campaign in South Africa] Zackie Achmat's voice in my head calling me an ultra-leftist for refusing to deal with institutions to effect change. Well, Zackie and TAC engage with their government on a daily basis and have created a national infrastructure to press for political change. I am not suggesting that there is no use for the UNGASS meeting, particularly when it is part of a comprehensive political response to the AIDS crisis. However, for many people, the UNGASS meeting has a role that is isolated from any other kind of political activity and has taken on a significance that it doesn't deserve. For me, the frenzy around the UNGASS meeting represented an anti-political moment. The UNGASS's role, its real contribution, to paraphrase [Indian writer/activist] Arundhati Roy, is to defuse political anger and blunt the edges of political resistance.

Reasons for the Current Crisis

How did we get here? Well, not to over-simplify, but I think that we've seen an NGO-ization of HIV/AIDS that has weakened or destroyed our ability to build a social movement to fight for our right to health, to be free of discrimination and violence, to the other services we need to stay alive and free from HIV infection. We've also seen people living with HIV/AIDS, sex workers, women, men-who-have-sex-with-men, ethnic minorities, young people, drug users who are also working in the field become essentialist monsters: that is they think and act as if the greater involvement of people with AIDS (GIPA) or their "vulnerable" group has a value in and of itself, as if they have some special purchase on knowledge or rights simply because of who they are instead of linking those rights to a responsibility to engage politically in a feminist, anti-racist, anti-homophobic, pro-sex, pro-harm reduction, and pro-poor struggle that links us in solidarity, in commonality with each other, with millions of other people for whom other struggles perhaps matter more than our own.

What would I love to see? Well, it would be great if we could have the chat that [American writer/activist] Vito Russo asked for in 1988. I'd like us to ask if the institutions and organizations we've built up are really working towards achieving political change or are actually stymieing it. How accountable are our NGOs to people living with HIV/AIDS and communities affected by the epidemic at the district level, the province, the country, the region, the planet? Are we creating institutions that seek to justify their own existence, their own organizational survival and expansion at the expense of challenging the powers-that-be: governments, UN agencies, drug companies, etc? Who is setting the agendas for our work? Are these agendas in the service of achieving specific, local political accountability or are they making calls for a more diffuse, generalized, international responsibility? Are we becoming carpetbaggers, itinerant technocrats, damn missionaries, toting our expertise around the globe trying to help people in other countries to solve their own problems or are we trying to promote local solutions to local problems by local people? Are we just talking about change, rather than mobilizing for it, trying to make it happen? Are we just managing change, trying to turn resistance into "a well-mannered, reasonable, salaried, 9-to-5 job," channeling the struggle into a three-day media event in New York City in May, a weeklong international AIDS conference in Toronto in August, and endless series of meetings, reports, conference calls and email exchanges?

Being Gay Is Not an Identity in Itself

I also want to stop talking about GIPA—the greater involvement of people living with HIV/AIDS. I am sick of GIPA and will not promote it any longer. Roy Cohn, the vicious, nasty, conservative asshole had AIDS and he was gay to boot. Roy Cohn sent Julius and Ethel Rosenberg to the electric chair and sat at the right hand of Senator Joseph McCarthy in the 1950s when he persecuted hundreds of decent Americans for communist sympathies, whether or not they had then or ever been members of the Communist Party. He was not part of my community. Do women want to claim [former British prime

65

minister] Margaret Thatcher as one of their own? Do gay men want to claim Ernst Rohm, commander of the Nazi storm troopers as a fellow fag? Do Africans want to claim [former Ugandan dictator] Idi Amin or [assassinated South African prime minister] Hendrik Verwoerd among their kin? If your own sense of your history or politics is based on biology, serostatus [HIV status], country of origin, gender, sexuality, well, get ready to get in bed with all of the folks mentioned above. This kind of identity politics excuses everything and accepts no political responsibility.

It's time we start asking each other: What are you doing to promote the reproductive and sexual rights of women; to fight rape and violence against women; to promote access to HIV/AIDS prevention, care and treatment, to education, to safe and affordable housing and other basic services regardless of gender, sexuality, ethnic origin, regardless of ability to pay? What are you doing to legalize methadone, buprenorphine, syringe exchange and reform drug and narcotics regulation, protect sex workers from harassment, ensure they have working conditions that don't endanger their health or well-being? What are you doing to ensure that young people get comprehensive information about sexuality, STIs [sexually transmitted infections] and HIV/AIDS?

Let's base our personal commitment to the fight against HIV/AIDS not on who we are, but what we do for others and not just for those who are like us, but those who are different in whichever way each of us chooses to categorize it. If we hold our organizations accountable, we have to hold ourselves accountable too.

So, I am one pissed off sister. I am angry at the epidemic, but angry about a machine we've created that drains the politics out of what is happening around us, that, in fact, fosters both an institutional and personal anti-politics that fuels the fires of HIV/AIDS. I don't know when we'll all get the chance to talk, but we need to have a conversation about where we're going and how we're going to get there. Otherwise, we'll see each other at the next UNGASS in another five years' time and realize we've been driving around in circles, never recognizing we've seen this all before, our journey hasn't even started and the car is, sadly, out of gas.

Christians Must Reach Out Without Bias

Amanda Grier

In this selection, the author urges Christian churches to reach out to HIV-positive people and abandon the stance that AIDS is a divine punishment for those who break religious laws. She argues that the church has to go beyond its call for abstinence and face modern life and AIDS with compassion, not rejection. Amanda Grier holds a BA in political science from Eastern University and an MA in international and European politics from the University of Edinburgh.

The recent observance of World AIDS Day provides those of us who are evangelical Christians with the opportunity to re-evaluate our role in the global fight against HIV/AIDS. After entering the battlefield shamefully late, Christians are now at the front lines. With the help of Christian advocacy, government funding and charitable giving have significantly increased. On the ground, Christian organizations like World Vision, Samaritan's Purse, MAP International, and World Relief contribute substantially to the prevention and treatment of HIV/AIDS and are well positioned internationally to inject assistance where it is needed most.

Unfortunately, there are many well-intentioned Christians who still see HIV/AIDS as God's punishment for homosexuality and sexual promiscuity and lobby fervently for abstinence and fidelity campaigns as the only response to HIV/AIDS. They believe that if people simply abstain from sex before marriage and remain faithful within marriage HIV/AIDS would be eradicated. This group of Christians has succeeded

Amanda Grier, "Are Christians Relevant in the AIDS Fight?" *Institute for Global Engagement*, February 10, 2006. © 2006 Institute for Global Engagement. Reproduced by permission.

in influencing US foreign aid policy towards HIV prevention. Consequently, foreign organizations and governments that promote abstinence programs and ignore the beneficial effects of condom distribution, prostitute outreach, and clean needle programs are favored with a disproportionate amount of support from the US government and Christian aid organizations.

Without delving into specific programs, I will speak more broadly about the limitations of programs that focus entirely on abstinence and fidelity. However, let me first say that I am not opposed to abstinence and fidelity programs nor deny their effectiveness. Instead, I am concerned about the deleterious effects of campaigns that ignore other effective methods of prevention. Campaigns or organizations that focus solely on abstinence and faithfulness in marriage leave the highest risk groups even more vulnerable to HIV infection and can compromise the relevancy of Christ's message of healing and forgiveness.

Relevance for American Youth

As a youth director for six years, I saw the limits of abstinence-only campaigns. I watched as teenagers sincerely committed themselves to abstinence one week, only to return with tears of defeat the next. Each young person was different. Some fell hard and often, others successfully refused sex, and still others stumbled once or twice. Faced with the realities of our fallen world, I have come to realize that people need every net available to resist sexual sin. One important net is the support of a Christian family and community. However, many kids lack this net. People make poor choices that have serious consequences because they do not have a relationship with Christ.

Let me juxtapose two young women I met during my time as a youth director. Mary and Martha both became sexually active at a young age. Mary, however, took precautions with condoms and birth control. Martha tried to abstain, but when she failed she became pregnant. Mary and Martha eventually accepted Christ, but Mary graduated from college while Martha is still trapped in an abusive relationship with her child's father.

When they lack comprehensive parental and community support, young people are vulnerable to unwanted pregnancy, abortion, or HIV infection. Abstinence-only campaigns do not resonate with many American youth because most teenagers lack the biblical foundation that makes the programs compelling. As a result, unbelieving teenagers hear a clear message of callous religiosity. Many believe that the stonewalling of condom distribution by Christians contributes to HIV infection, unwanted pregnancy, and abortion. As teenagers and their loved ones deal with issues like rape, drug addiction, alcohol abuse, unwanted pregnancy, and homosexuality, they rarely respond to a message of condemnation and fear. However, I have witnessed lives transformed when Christ's message of forgiveness and healing is internalized. Most who remain sexually pure do so because of their love for Christ rather than a fear of AIDS. As God's messengers, we must constantly reevaluate the appropriateness of our actions or risk becoming part of the problem.

Relevance for Women

Although the message of abstinence and fidelity as the only defense against AIDS is unsuccessful in reaching the most vulnerable in the United States, there are many Christians successfully advancing it abroad. These one-dimensional campaigns appear to be replacing successful holistic action in countries like Uganda with dangerous consequences. When exported, abstinence-only platforms often fail to accommodate the various cultural differences and deep gender disempowerment present in the hardest hit regions. Similar to the US, programs that only promote abstinence hurt the most vulnerable.

Internationally, the two most vulnerable groups to HIV infection are those who engage in risky behavior and those who lack control over the risky behavior of their partners. The first group is widely understood. Those who engage in unprotected sex with multiple partners, inject drug[s], and [engage in] prostitution put themselves at incredible risk for HIV infection. They are unlikely to stop their unhealthy behavior for fear of AIDS because they already demonstrate a high tolerance for dangerous choices. However, they respond well to unobtrusive condom campaigns. Withholding access to condoms, as some Christians propose, can prove fatal.

Women Are at a High Risk

The second high-risk group is the often monogamous sexual partners of those practicing the above-mentioned risky behavior. In other words, women, and ultimately their children, are extremely vulnerable to HIV. According to the 2004 UN AIDS [the Joint United Nations Programme on HIV/AIDS] report, most women who contract the disease do so from their unfaithful and much older husbands. These women can then pass the virus onto their children either during pregnancy, birth, or breast-feeding. Consequently, every minute, one child dies from an AIDS-related disease and another child becomes infected with HIV. Furthermore, girls are disproportionately affected due to societal inequalities that force them and their families to rely upon the sexual desires of older men.

It is now generally accepted that the primary cause of high infection rates among women and their children is societal gender discrimination. As long as women endure widespread rape and violence they lack the option of abstinence. Therefore in the struggle against AIDS, we must also combat the disempowerment of women that allows impunity for abuse, economic hardship, and dependence upon abusers.

Until gender equality is achieved, condom distribution is the next best tool against the spread of HIV. In fact, according to the 2004 UN AIDS Report, when male partners simply used condoms, female risk of HIV infection decreased. Condom usage, however, is only one short-term tool. More campaigns must focus on male accountability and respect for women as people rather than consumable goods. The most effective programs are those which employ comprehensive strategies that effectively combat female disempowerment, discourage risky sexual behavior, encourage abstinence and fidelity, and provide access to treatment and condoms.

The difficulty Western Christians have in understanding the gender dynamics in many parts of the world has contributed to favoritism toward abstinence-only campaigns that focus primarily on female sexuality. We assume that women, like men, have control over their sexuality. As AIDS spreads rapidly among faithful wives, the reality for many women is that the institution of marriage repeatedly fails to protect women from rape, violence, and HIV infection. Monogamous women are now the highest risk group internationally. Men who visit prostitutes, have multiple wives, inherit wives from relatives, and inject drugs place their wives and children at risk. Marriage is promoted as a safe place for women, but this illusion can contribute to their death. Abstinence and fidelity-only campaigns are unrealistic in a world that does not know Christ and treats women like consumable products.

Christ's Example

During his earthly ministry, Jesus provided numerous illustrations of love toward others, especially sinners and our enemies. His patience is unending when confronted with sinners and the sick but shockingly short with Pharisees, a group that worked diligently to follow God's law. In our campaigns against HIV/AIDS we must follow the example of Christ by finding effective strategies that relieve suffering and offer forgiveness. Study for yourself Christ's response to sexual impurity and measure that against your own.

In John 9, Jesus explains one origin of suffering when he heals a man born blind, "this happened so that the work of God might be displayed in his life." The healing of this blind man led to an intense theological debate regarding the causal relationship between suffering and sin. However, the lesson is made clear in the proclamation of the healed man, "One thing I do know. I was blind and now I see!" What a powerful message Christ gave us to share with the world! When Christians provide proper treatment and prevention of HIV/AIDS we send a daily message of forgiveness and healing to a hurting world dealing with a global pandemic.

Denial Is Not an Option

Like many diseases, the spread of AIDS is the outward manifestation of larger social infirmities. Christians are not immune from blame. Thus, we must diligently examine Christian culpability in the spread of AIDS. Condoms and clean needles have been proven to save lives and slow the spread of HIV in some contexts and therefore deserve consideration. As donors, activists, organizations, government workers and laypersons, our global strategy against AIDS should be one of intelligent compassion, where the vilest sinners are healed and all available tools are utilized.

Combating the AIDS Epidemic in India

Scott Baldauf

Many people in India, especially in rural regions, have little knowledge of what AIDS is and how it spreads. In this viewpoint, volunteers describe the challenges they have faced on a march throughout the country in an effort to educate Indians about HIV/AIDS. Scott Baldauf is a staff writer for The Christian Science Monitor.

There's something timeless about the arrival of a street-theater group in the hustle-bustle bazaar of a small town like Palwal. The actors arrive, shouting, beating two-sided *dholak* drums, and donning kitschy costumes of golden tinsel.

A crowd naturally gathers. And then the actors pull a fast one. This is no mere entertainment. This is an educational program conducted by AIDS Walk for Life, a village to village tour by volunteers who are walking part—or all—of a more than 4,200-mile circuit around India. Their goal: to raise awareness about a disease that has already made India the country with the second-highest number of people living with HIV. The tour will conclude in Delhi [on] World AIDS Day [December 1].

"In a country where so many people still know so little about the disease, the walk has been a dramatic and effective way to spread awareness," says Henry Alderfer of Project Concern International in India, the group sponsoring the walk.

To the surprise of the organizers, the vast majority of the walkers have been with the project from the get-go, walking mile after mile, bursting with energy each morning as they enter villages with banners and bullhorns, shouting, "Join hands together, defeat AIDS."

Following the Highways

The walkers follow the national highway system—one of the key transmission routes for the virus. The highest concentrations of HIV cases are in the south and west of the country, in states where many working-age men travel abroad as laborers. From these states, the virus has spread along highways. Truckers and laborers pick it up from commercial sex workers, and take it to their wives, who sometimes pass it to their newborns.

"People to people, we have had a large effect," says Hemant Singh, a dance teacher from Delhi, who has been with the AIDS Walk from the start. "If you stay at home, you can't do anything about the problem."

Bharat Bhushan, logistics head from the state of Bihar, says the more powerful lessons come from teaching by example. In the state of Andhra Pradesh, they persuaded a family to welcome back an HIV positive family member. The family feared that HIV could be transmitted by touch, and worried also about the stigma of the disease. One AIDS walker solved this problem by hugging the person with HIV.

"They were afraid to touch his hands, to eat food with him," says Mr. Bhushan. "We said, 'See, I'm not infected and I'm doing this. You are their family members. When you discriminate against your own family member, then what will others do?'"

An Effective Effort, but Still a Serious Problem

Efforts to raise awareness are just one of many ways that communities and agencies in India are meeting the challenge of AIDS, an epidemic that has largely spread through unsafe sex, lack of hygiene, and illicit drug use. Yet there are recent signs that awareness programs like the AIDS Walk are some of the most effective methods for stopping the spread of AIDS and the HIV virus.

"Arghh, that was the wrong tooth," the man says.

The doctor pulls out a syringe—a massive plunger he has already used on several other patients—and the man cringes. "Is that for a buffalo or a man?"

At the end, an educator steps forward to give the moral. "AIDS doesn't spread only by sex, it also can spread through dirty needles at the doctor's office. Make sure that your doctor always uses a clean syringe."

A Practitioner's Perspective on AIDS

Alice Rosenberg, interviewed by Ken Adelman

Alice Rosenberg, who coordinates HIV/AIDS outpatient care at the National Institutes of Health's [NIH] Clinical Center in Bethesda, Maryland, reflects on her profession, the stress involved in caring for the fatally ill, her outlook on life, and the future of AIDS in an interview by Ken Adelman. Adelman has been conducting interviews for his What I've Learned *column in the* Washingtonian *since 1988.*

Ken Adelman: *Is AIDS a chronic disease now?*

Alice Rosenberg: It's become more of one since treatments have become so effective. Nonetheless, most people with AIDS now will die from it or its complications. The lifespan of someone with AIDS used to be 15 years after initial infection. New medicines extend this. They can extend good quality of life, but sometimes they extend the part of life with the highest occurrence of complications.

How well or how long life is extended depends on how faithfully patients take their medicine and whether they develop secondary problems. Many are also heroin addicts or alcoholics—neither of which encourages rigorous compliance. Some are infected with other diseases as well.

Is there a false sense of security because of the advances in treatment?

When AIDS medicines called protease inhibitors were first available in the mid-1990s and the initial results were so positive, yes, there was a flood of media reports that the worst was

Ken Adelman, "HIV/AIDS: Interview With NIH's Alice Rosenberg," *The Washingtonian*, December 1, 2005. © 2005 Washingtonian Magazine, Inc. Reproduced by permission of the author.

over. This led to increased-risk behavior. Many thought, "All I have to do is take some medicine and I'll be okay."

It's since been demonstrated that this medicine isn't so easy to take. It's expensive, it can be toxic, and resistance frequently occurs.

Who's getting AIDS now [in 2005]?

More women, for sure. When I started at Whitman-Walker [clinics in the D.C. area] in the early '90s, 7 percent of my patients were women. When I left in '99, it was 24 percent. Now it's a little higher than that.

AIDS has very much become a heterosexual illness. Heterosexuals are at risk each time they have unprotected sex with a person they don't know—and often with someone they do. The receptive partner is far more likely to get infected; a female is more likely to be infected by a male.

Many gay men are back in sex clubs. Young gay men contracting HIV weren't around for the first wave. They didn't know the 30- or 40-year-olds infected then, most of whom are dead now. And the press now hypes the treatments, which drives precautions down further.

I used to talk to high-school kids constantly. They all think they're immune. Their friends are young and healthy. And they're not particularly promiscuous. They don't understand that it doesn't take much to get infected. [They don't realize that] they're not sleeping with just one individual— they're sleeping with every person who ever slept with that individual.

A few years ago, when I toured high schools talking about AIDS, I was told not to use the word "condom." I had to say "latex product," and only when speaking of family planning.

A group called Metro TeenAIDS is now very active in doing outreach to area high schools.

Where is the incidence of AIDS rising?

The number of young gay men getting infected is approaching the levels of the mid-'80s. Besides an increased incidence among women, there's been a steep rise among minorities. This increase is partly because there are more cases and partly because there's better reporting of cases.

The statistics are tough to get accurate. Rate of incidence doesn't necessarily equal rate of treatment, as there are eight to ten years between infection and the occurrence of symptoms. Current estimates for Washington show that as many as 30 percent of people infected with HIV are unaware that they're HIV-positive.

In general, many of the people seeking treatment are males 15 to 35 years old, and they don't adhere well to treatment. They're not accustomed to complying with rules. When they do, the medicine doesn't make them feel better. They get nauseated—which isn't positive reinforcement.

But isn't it a death sentence not to take the medicines?

Sure, but that's over the long term. These people aren't thinking long term. Many have dealt with drug addiction, alcoholism, and poverty before contracting HIV. Many have lost their jobs since becoming sick. They have no money and go on welfare.

We help all of our patients follow their regimens by simple steps like giving them cab fare to go to the doctor, or childcare if they're mothers. I have a patient now—a young woman who's HIV-positive. Her child's positive, too. The mother sends the kid off to school, and the girl has diarrhea on the bus and returns home. That mother won't make it to her own doctor's appointment that day.

One of our key medications causes nightmares and vivid dreams. These patients wake up feeling like they haven't slept. So we schedule the medication better. Such adjustments take a lot of phone calls and support.

I tell patients: "Come in and see me. When you feel you want to kill yourself, just come in. Spend the day with us here. Maybe you'll feel a bit better."

I warn them that they're going to hear from me and hear from me and hear from me. One of my patients, a guy whose wife also had AIDS and died recently, told me that if he ever gets married again, he'll do so during [the Jewish holiday of] Passover because he knows I'm gone then and won't be bothering him.

What works in prevention?

Condoms. I beg providers for cases of them. I want them readily available—hoping that if someone has them, that person will use them.

Condoms should be available in schools. Making them so doesn't create promiscuity. It's embarrassing for kids to go to the drugstore to buy condoms. We've got to accept that high-school kids have sex. Using condoms is the only real way of preventing the spread of HIV.

You have no faith in abstinence?

It's beyond naïve to think that abstinence will work. You'd be counting on kids not to do the natural thing. A small core of devout Christian kids might buy that, but not the vast majority. Certainly not college kids, who have a newfound freedom and space to have sex.

What's a common reaction when you tell young people they're HIV-positive?

Most cry. They're stunned: "I can't believe this has happened to me. How am I going to tell my family? My friends?"

I suggest, "Perhaps you should wait to tell anybody until you're used to it yourself." This gives a person a chance to feel some sense of control as well as time to determine what to say and to whom. That might take a week, sometimes a month. I say, "Get your head together first, however long that takes. And don't have unprotected sex."

After being told they're HIV-positive, some can't wait to get out the door. I won't hear from them for a month or more. They're in denial. Others say, "I just knew it was going to happen to me"—as if they had nothing to do with it.

I ask them to backtrack: "When do you think you got infected? What happened since then? You need to be in touch with those people." They have a responsibility to tell their sexual contacts. I can help with that process if necessary.

How does someone with AIDS end up at NIH's Clinical Center instead of at a local clinic like Whitman-Walker?

The center includes a 242-bed hospital with patients from around Washington. New patients hear about us by word of mouth. Another part of the Clinical Center is the much larger research clinic. It gets referrals through primary-care physicians and patients themselves who are investigating new treatment protocols on the Web. These patients come from all over the world.

Treating people with AIDS costs a lot of money.

Oh, my God, yes. Each patient costs tens of thousands a year. Each takes a combination of three to five medicines to treat AIDS, and most will require two or three more to prevent other infections or minimize the recurrence of infections. Many patients—including poor ones—get help from government programs.

We don't start any treatment until a patient's immune system has deteriorated to roughly a third of its normal capacity. According to our best information, starting treatment earlier doesn't help.

What's it like to be with people at the end of their lives?

I share a unique intimacy with someone living his or her last days on earth. Once they have their financial affairs in order, it's my job to get the family to be supportive.

Patients tell me how they want to be buried and remembered. Most have no recent pictures of themselves. When I ask for a good picture, they show me one from five or six years ago.

Many worry about having trouble breathing and being in pain. We have medicines and other ways to keep them comfortable. They come to understand they don't have to be afraid.

Some ask to hear their favorite music or a poem. If a friend stops by, they want to hear that person's voice. They ask me to position their friends outside the door, and they talk to them from there. Their bodies are wasted—down to 80 or 90 pounds—and they don't want to be remembered like that.

What do they want you to do?

Talk to them. Keep them comfortable. If they have trouble breathing, I'll get them oxygen. If they're in pain, I'll get them morphine.

Do many talk about God?

Not much. After five or eight years of battling AIDS, most talk of God is gone. A few go back to Jesus, but most feel nothing spiritual after being so sick for so long. They've lost confidence that God is looking after them.

Many choose to be cremated, since they don't want to remain the way they are. They get very involved in where their ashes go. Some have their funeral before dying. They want to hear the eulogies, to hear what people think of them.

At the very end, rarely do they resist death. Most have little strength left. They go gently.

What have you learned from helping them die?

Among gay men with AIDS, it's how supportive the gay community is. When one of them gets sick, they circle the wagons. They pick the guy up, carry him to the bathroom, make sure he eats and gets what he needs. The strength and character of that community is remarkable.

I was stunned by the lack of the medical establishment's response to this illness early on. The federal government was slow to pick up on the need and offer support, but it's much better now. AIDS is now a disability, so someone contracting it becomes eligible for government support. That was a while in coming.

What have you learned about treating people with AIDS?

How clever this virus is. It mutates around everything put in its way. When we started with the drug AZT, the virus quickly went around that. We constantly need new drug combinations. We now have 23 anti-HIV medications.

There won't be a vaccine soon. Anything injected to prevent the virus from replicating will prompt the virus to go around that and replicate.

I've learned how unaccepting people are of HIV and AIDS. They don't want to hear about it. Few can accept how susceptible their children are—even good kids in Ivy League schools.

What have you learned about family reactions?

In the case of gay men, that they're mostly abysmal. I've called many parents to tell them, "Your boy is very ill. You know he's gay. Now I must tell you he has AIDS and he would like to see you."

Many respond that they won't have anything to do with him. So we end our conversation by my saying, "I'm awfully sorry, since your involvement could really help your son."

Sometimes a mother will call back months later. I'll often have to say, "Your boy is not with us anymore."

The mom then becomes weepy and remorseful. But where has she been for the past five years, when her son had no money, no help, and was asking me to care for him?

Brothers tend to have trouble with the gay thing. Sisters are much better. Sisters stick. They don't have the same baggage as parents or brothers. Often the family support comes from the sister.

Why do you do this work?

After staying home for 20 years raising children, I wanted to return to nursing—but only where I was really needed. I didn't need a swanky downtown office.

Isn't it depressing?

Not for me. It's a privilege to help people die with dignity.

What do they say?

Not much, since usually we're both crying by then.

What have you learned about life?

Do what you really want to do. And make every day count, because you don't know when it'll end. Things change very, very quickly.

The Past, Present, and Future of AIDS Research

Robert Gallo, interviewed by Jonathan Bor

In this interview, Robert Gallo, who discovered the virus that causes AIDS, reflects on the past, on the difficulties of AIDS research, and on new possibilities of finding effective treatments for the disease. Gallo heads the University of Maryland's Institute of Human Virology. Jonathan Bor is a Baltimore Sun *staff writer.*

Jonathan Bor: *Twenty years ago, did you ever imagine that the disease would become the pandemic it has: 20 million lives claimed, nearly 40 million infected today across the world?*

Robert Gallo: In some respects yes, and in other respects no. By the time we submitted our papers [reporting the discovery] in March of 1984 for publication, we were beginning to collaborate with people who were applying our newly developed blood tests. So we know it was becoming really widespread.

A dramatic example of that occurred when a post-doc[toral student] of ours from Tokyo obtained serum from hemophiliacs receiving Factor 8, a blood-derived product. In March or April of 1984, nobody was positive.

Then, a few months later, after using blood products from the U.S. and Europe, we found 20 percent of the hemophiliacs were positive. So we had no doubt this was going to become a global epidemic.

What we didn't expect is the uniformity—that without today's therapy it was almost completely fatal. Very few microbes kill virtually everybody they infect.

On a similar note, did you imagine that you and others in the forefront of AIDS research would still be pursuing a cure and a vaccine 20 years later?

Jonathan Bor, "20 Years Later, Gallo Looks at AIDS, Future," *Baltimore Sun*, November 12, 2004. Copyright © 2004, The Baltimore Sun. Used by permission.

No, I did not. I thought I'd be back full time with cancer research. But also, I certainly thought that this was a virus that wouldn't go away. To make an analogy, what's worse—the plague or this? It depends on how you look at the world. The plague really rushes through like a tornado, killing things in its path, but then rather quickly disappears. But we knew the nature of retroviruses [a class of viruses that includes HIV and hepatitis B and C]—they don't go away.

So I knew that if we didn't do anything about it that this wasn't going to go away. But I expected that medical science would solve it with a preventive vaccine by now. I didn't expect any cure therapeutically. Remember, we didn't have any chemical therapy against any other viruses except very toxic drugs that weren't very effective.

But the surprise has been the wonderful therapies that became available. . . . So we thought there would be little therapy but success with a protective vaccine, and it turned out to be quite the opposite. On that, our instincts were completely wrong, and the vast majority of people thought exactly the same thing.

One obstacle to creating an AIDS vaccine is that the virus mutates rapidly, making it a moving target. At your institute, Timothy Fouts and Anthony DeVico have developed a vaccine designed to elicit antibodies against a variety of AIDS strains. How far along is this vaccine and how close to human trials?

We are in the final stages of discussions with a major pharmaceutical company. I would expect everything by the end of the year [2004] to be done. We'll do research. The company would fund the research and make the product. It won't be more than one to two years for the first phase [of clinical trials, which measure safety]. . . . But I don't know all the social, political and even scientific [hurdles], like production, production costs, working out this agreement and that agreement. It takes so frustratingly long.

The real point of this, it's a big mistake to go into vaccine research when you're in middle age—better when you're in your 20s. Then, one of the problems is that a young person can't get funded for research like this.

Do you think you'll have a chance to see a vaccine?

[Laughing]. I don't know. I've got to stay healthy.

Since creating the Institute of Human Virology [in 1996], has your work taken any surprising turns? Has the focus turned out differently than you imagined?

In one substantive way: the international angle, the amount of global public health. If you told me 10 years ago that I'd be in Russia related to public health issues and in China to form collaborations with the Chinese [version of the] CDC [Centers for Disease Control and Prevention], to get them to commit to the problem with maximum scientific force, and [that our group would be] greatly involved in Africa, I would have been surprised.

When you first came to Baltimore, you said that the city— with one of the highest HIV infection rates in the country— offered a perfect laboratory for research into treatments and vaccines. Has this proved to be the case?

Absolutely, a very strong yes. On a very practical level, we have the patient population to be able to help and be able to collectively learn more.

We've seen the evolution of drug resistance, the problem of compliance, the need for basic research. We see firsthand the extent of [drug] toxicity and what areas we need to work on. And we've learned, for instance, that we can give a rest period for people on the drugs. We've had the privilege of seeing people who didn't get any care before get care now. We've seen people who were undertreated and at death's door . . . come back. All of this is more than we could have hoped for.

The drug cocktails that have been in use for several years have enabled people to live much longer, free of serious symp-

toms. Yet they are not a cure. Do you see anything on the horizon that would wipe out the virus, never to return?

No, I do not. That gets into the extraordinary molecular biology [of HIV infection]. You've got to sense out every cell that harbors silent genes of the virus. There are many cells, though their percentages are small, that harbor these genes in a silent form. Having drugs that can find the genes and kill these cells is out of our reach in the foreseeable future.

[Gallo, however, said he is excited about a new class of experimental drugs, called entry inhibitors, that block the virus from getting inside cells of the immune system]. They are a wonderful new class. Remember, we have increasing resistance to the currently used drugs. Until "pharma" [the pharmaceutical industry] comes up with more and more drugs, resistance is going to be a problem.

This year [2004], a consortium led by the institute and Catholic Relief Services was awarded a $335 million federal grant to deliver AIDS drugs in Africa and the Caribbean through faith-based groups there. The grant covers five years. Why the emphasis on religious groups?

It's important for the general reader to know that it's not limited to faith-based groups, but we are working with faith-based groups that have been on the ground in Africa for a long time and have a track record of being trusted and doing good work. . . . [These] groups are better than governments in getting to the people. People would have to say, 'Why not?'

Does this mean the programs will be promoting abstinence-only prevention, which would mean not talking about the role of condoms in blocking prevention?

The answer to that is a simple no. Look, Uganda is the most successful program in the world. Yes, condoms are available, but they also preached monogamy—not to cheat on your partners. Clearly, they make part of the program that sex can transmit the virus and that an important part of prevention is staying with your partner.

Since coming to Baltimore, have there been any major pleasant surprises or disappointments?

On the pleasant side, there is no question that Baltimore is a wonderful City . . . much more than I would have anticipated. People are original, interesting. I have season tickets for the opera; now I have season tickets for the Ravens. We're a city of characters. The University of Maryland also has many major pluses.

On disappointments, yes, but I won't comment.

Organizations to Contact

The editors have compiled the following list of organizations concerned with the issues debated in this book. The descriptions are derived from materials provided by the organizations. All have publications or information available for interested readers. The list was compiled on the date of publication of the present volume; the information provided here may change. Be aware that many organizations take several weeks or longer to respond to inquiries, so allow as much time as possible.

Adolescent AIDS Program (AAP)
Children's Hospital at Montefiore Medical Center
111 E. 210th St., Bronx, NY   10467
(718) 882-0232 • fax: (718) 882-0432
e-mail: info@adolescentaids.org
Web site: www.adolescentaids.org

The AAP serves as a local and national resource for those living with HIV/AIDS; adolescents aged thirteen to twenty-four who are at risk for HIV infection; health-care providers who treat adolescents living with or at risk for HIV infection; and lesbian, gay, bisexual, transgender, or questioning adolescents, their families, and caregivers. The AAP offers comprehensive news and information in Web articles and minimagazines.

AIDS Coalition to Unleash Power (ACT UP)
332 Bleecker St., Suite G-5, New York, NY   10014
(212) 642-5499 • fax: (212) 642-5499
e-mail: actupny@panix.com
Web site: www.actupny.org

ACT UP was formed in 1987 in New York. Members believe that AIDS is a political and social issue and work to heighten awareness of the illness and how it is treated in the United States and worldwide. ACT UP members meet with government officials, hold protests, distribute and post medical information, and publish many materials, including the handbook *Women and AIDS*.

AIDSinfo
PO Box 6303, Rockville, MD   20849-6303
(800) HIV-0440 (1-800-448-0440) • fax: (301) 519-6616
e-mail: contactus@aidsinfo.nih.gov.
Web site: aidsinfo.nih.gov

AIDSinfo provides information in Spanish and English on HIV/AIDS treatment, prevention, and research. Its Web site contains information about vaccines, clinical trials, and drugs, and offers links to articles and other organizations.

AIDS National Interfaith Network (ANIN)
110 Maryland Ave. NE, Suite 504, Washington, DC   20002
(202) 546-0807 • fax: (202) 546-5103

ANIN is a coalition of religious organizations whose goal is to see that everyone affected by AIDS receives compassion, respect, care, and assistance. The network opposes threats to the civil liberties of AIDS patients, including violations of confidentiality and all forms of prejudice and discrimination. Among the organization's publications are the handbooks *America Living with AIDS* and *AIDS and Your Religious Community*.

American Civil Liberties Union (ACLU)
132 W. Forty-third St., New York, NY   10036
(212) 944-9800 • fax: (212) 869-9065
Web site: www.aclu.org

The ACLU champions the rights set forth in the Declaration of Independence and the U.S. Constitution. It opposes any actions, including testing and contact tracing, that might endanger the civil rights of people with AIDS. The ACLU's numerous publications include the book *The Rights of Lesbians and Gay Men*, which contains a section on discrimination against people with AIDS, and the briefing paper "AIDS and Civil Liberties."

Family Research Council (FRC)
700 Thirteenth St. NW, Suite 500, Washington, DC   20005
(202) 393-2100 • fax: (202) 393-2134
Web site: www.frc.org

The FRC believes in strengthening the institutions of marriage and the family. It considers AIDS to be part of a larger, broader social problem that can be combated through promoting primary prevention methods, such as sexual abstinence until marriage and monogamy within marriage. The FRC publishes various position papers regarding AIDS policy, including "The Social Impact of the AIDS Lobby," "How to Overhaul AIDS Spending," and "Will Needle Exchange Save America's Future?"

Focus on the Family
8605 Explorer Dr., Colorado Springs, CO   80920
(719) 531-3400 • fax: (719) 531-3331

Focus on the Family is a Christian organization that seeks to strengthen the traditional family in America. It promotes abstinence from sex until marriage as a way for teenagers to avoid AIDS, and it advocates monogamy within marriage. It publishes a variety of materials, including the booklet *AIDS: Facts vs. Fiction*, the information sheet "AIDS Resources," and the monthly magazine *Focus on the Family*.

Gay Men's Health Crisis (GMHC)
129 W. Twentieth St., New York, NY   10011-0022
(212) 807-6655 • fax: (212) 337-3656

The GMHC, founded in 1982, is the oldest and largest AIDS network. It provides support services, education, and advocacy for men, women, and children with AIDS. The group publishes the monthly AIDS therapy journal *Treatment Issues* as well as a variety of position papers.

The Hetrick-Martin Institute (HMI)
2 Astor Pl., New York, NY   10003

(212) 674-2400 • fax: (212) 674-8650

The HMI offers a broad range of social services to gay and lesbian adolescents and their families as well as to teenagers at high risk of AIDS. It provides direct services to gay and lesbian youth, including group and individual counseling and referral, an outreach service to homeless youth, and education on human sexuality and AIDS. The HMI publishes the quarterly newsletter *HMI Report Card*.

Mothers' Voices
165 W. Forty-sixth St., Suite 1310, New York, NY 10036
(212) 730-2777 • fax: (212) 730-4378

Mothers' Voices is composed of mothers concerned about AIDS. It works for AIDS education to prevent the transmission of HIV, the promotion of safer sexual behavior, research for better treatments and a cure, and compassion for every person living with HIV and AIDS. The group publishes the newsletter *Speaking from the Heart* three times a year and the policy statement *Expanded Bio-Medical Research*.

National AIDS Fund
1400 Eye St. NW, Suite 1220, Washington, DC 20005-2208
(202) 408-4848 • fax: (202) 408-1818

The fund is dedicated to eliminating HIV as a major health and social problem. It works with the public and private sectors to provide care and prevent new infections through advocacy, grant-making, research, and education in communities and the workplace. The fund's numerous publications include the booklet *The ADA, FMLA, and AIDS: An Employer's Guide to Managing HIV Infected Employees* and *A Generation at Risk: A Background Report on HIV Prevention and Youth*.

The Rockford Institute
934 N. Main St., Rockford, IL 61103
(815) 964-5053 • fax: (815) 965-1826

The institute calls for rebuilding moral values and recovering the traditional American family. It believes that AIDS is a symptom of the decline of the traditional family and that only by supporting traditional families and traditional moral be-havior will America rid itself of AIDS. The institute publishes the monthlies *Chronicles, Family in America,* and *Religion & Society Report.*

For Further Research

Books

Elias K. Bongmba, *Facing a Pandemic: The African Church and the Crisis of HIV/AIDS.* Waco, TX: Baylor University Press, 2007.

Steve Chimombo, *AIDS Artists and Authors: Popular Responses to the Epidemic: 1985–2006.* Zomba, Malawi: WASI Publications, 2007.

Helen Epstein, *The Invisible Cure: Africa, the West, and the Fight Against AIDS.* New York: Farrar, Straus & Giroux, 2007.

Hung Y. Fan, Ross F. Conner, Luis P. Villarreal, *AIDS: Science and Society.* Sudbury, MA: Jones and Bartlett, 2007.

Allen Gifford, Kate Long, Diana Laurent, and Virginia Gonzalez, *Living Well with HIV and AIDS.* 2nd ed. Boulder, CO: Bull, 2000.

Matthew Gutmann, *Fixing Men: Sex, Birth Control, and AIDS in Mexico.* Berkeley and Los Angeles: University of California Press, 2007.

Marvin Kitzerow, *The AIDS Indictment.* MRKCO, 2000.

Jay A. Levy, *HIV and the Pathogenesis of AIDS.* Washington, DC: ASM, 2007.

National Intelligence Council Staff, *The Global Infectious Disease Threat and Its Implications for the United States.* Washington, DC: U.S. Central Intelligence Agency, 2000.

Robert L. Ostergard Jr., ed., *HIV/AIDS and the Threat to National and International Security.* New York: Palgrave Macmillan, 2007.

Mark Padilla, *Caribbean Pleasure Industry: Tourism, Sexuality, and AIDS in the Dominican Republic.* Chicago: University of Chicago Press, 2007.

Hakan Seckinelgin, *International Politics of HIV/AIDS: Global Disease—Local Pain.* New York: Routledge, 2008.

Shawn Smallman, *The AIDS Pandemic in Latin America.* Chapel Hill: University of North Carolina Press, 2007.

Corinne Squire, *HIV in South Africa: Talking About the Big Thing.* New York: Routledge, 2007.

Eileen Stillwaggon, *AIDS and the Ecology of Poverty.* New York: Oxford University Press, 2006.

Mario Taguiwalo, *A Review of ASEP-Assisted HIV Prevention Activities in 3 Cities.* Manila, the Philippines: PATH and AIDS Surveillance and Education Project, 2000.

UNAIDS, *Report on the Global HIV/AIDS Epidemic.* Geneva, Switzerland: UNAIDS, 2004.

———, *AIDS Epidemic Update: December 2003.* Geneva: UNAIDS, 2003.

———, Report on the Global HIV/AIDS Epidemic. Geneva: UNAIDS, 2002.

UNICEF/UNAIDS/WHO, *Young People and HIV/AIDS: Opportunity in Crisis.* Geneva: UNICEF/UNAIDS/WHO, 2002.

UNICEF/UNAIDS/The Synergy Project, *Children on the Brink, 2002: A Joint Report on Orphan Estimates and Program Strategies.* Geneva: UNICEF/UNAIDS, 2002.

Alex de Waal, *AIDS and Power: Why There Is No Political Crisis—Yet.* New York: Zed Books, in association with the International African Institute, 2006.

World Health Organization/UNAIDS *WHO/UNAIDS, Technical Consultation on Voluntary HIV Counselling and*

Testing: Models for Implementation and Strategies for the Scaling Up of VCT Services. Geneva: WHO/UNAIDS, 2001.

Periodicals

Mary Travis Basset, "Ensuring a Public Health Impact of Programs to Reduce HIV Transmission from Mothers to Infants: The Place of Voluntary Counseling and Testing," *American Journal of Public Health*, March 2002.

Lisanne Brown et al., "Interventions to Reduce HIV/AIDS Stigma: What Have We Learned?" *AIDS Education and Prevention*, 2003.

Joanne Busza, "Promoting the Positive: Responses to Stigma and Discrimination in Southeast Asia," *AIDS Care*, 2001.

Centers for Disease Control and Prevention, "Cases of HIV infection and AIDS in the United States, 2004," *HIV/AIDS Surveillance Report*, 2005.

——, "Number of Persons Tested for HIV—United States," *Morbidity and Mortality Weekly Report*, December 3, 2004.

Anthony S. Fauci, "Beyond Eradication," interview by Lark Lands, *POZ*, March 2000.

Robin Fox, "Tanzanian AIDS Project Works Towards 'Good Things for Young People," *Lancet*, May 13, 2000.

Joel E. Gallant, "Strategies for Long-Term Success in the Treatment of HIV Infections," *Journal of the American Medical Association*, March 8, 2000.

Helene D. Gayle, "Still Our Brothers," *Amsterdam (NY) News*, February 10, 2000.

Degu Jerene, Aschalew Endale, and Bernt Lindtjørn, "Acceptability of HIV Counseling and Testing Among Tuberculosis Patients in South Ethiopia," *BMC International Health and Human Rights*, May 2007.

Seth Kalichman and Leickness Simbayi, "Traditional Beliefs About the Cause of AIDS and AIDS-Related Stigma in South Africa," *AIDS Care*, 2004.

Gladys Mabunda, "Voluntary HIV Counseling and Testing: Knowledge and Practices in a Rural South African Village," *Journal of Transcultural Nursing*, 2006.

Suzanne Maman et al., "HIV-Positive Women Report More Lifetime Partner Violence: Findings from a Voluntary Counseling and Testing Clinic in Dar es Salaam, Tanzania," *American Journal of Public Health*, August 2002.

PATH (Program for Appropriate Technology in Health), "Preventing HIV/AIDS in Low-Resource Settings," *Outlook*, May 2001.

Jane Saunders, "Bipolar Disorder and HIV," *South-African-Psychiatry-Review*, February 2002.

Leickness Simbayi et al., "Behavioural Responses of South African Youth to the HIV/AIDS Epidemic: A Nationwide Survey," *AIDS Care*, 2004.

UNAIDS, "An Overview of HIV/AIDS-Related Stigma and Discrimination," Fact Sheet. October 2001.

———, "HIV Voluntary Counselling and Testing: A Gateway to Prevention and Care," UNAIDS Case Study, June 2002.

Index